Managing your Competencies

'He who does not know where he wants to go will never get there!'

'He who does not know where he is does not know how far he still has to go!'

Managing your Competencies

Personal Development Plan

Roel Grit

Roelie Guit

Nico van der Sijde

Second edition

Noordhoff Uitgevers Groningen | Houten

Cover design: G2K designers Groningen/Amsterdam
Book design: Ebel Kuipers, Sappemeer

Kindly address comments and remarks on this and other publications to:
Noordhoff Uitgevers bv, Afdeling Hoger Onderwijs, Antwoordnummer 13,
9700 VB Groningen, e-mail: info@noordhoff.nl

0 1 2 3 4 5 / 12 11 10 09 08

© 2008 Noordhoff Uitgevers bv Groningen/Houten, The Netherlands.

ISBN 978-90-01-76363-3
NUR 143

Introduction

In higher education so-called competency-orientated teaching has become an important objective. The book *Managing your Competencies* is a workbook with assignments aimed at helping students in higher education institutions to gain insight into the development of their own competencies. A competency is a combination of knowledge, skills and attitude needed for proper functioning in a given professional situation.

Although each training course requires its own competencies, the book *Managing your Competencies* can be used for various courses within higher education, from technical and teacher training colleges to art schools and information technology courses.

In many studies, students are required to set up a so-called personal development plan (PDP). The aim of this book is to help students to arrive independently at a PDP through assignments and exercises. The PDP contains an inventory of the competencies already achieved by the student and describes competencies still to be achieved. If a PDP is properly set up and executed, competencies will have been acquired that the student must possess as a professional starting out. We have consciously chosen not to write a book of written exercises. That is why via a website an accompanying program is available, containing the PDP Toolbox. The PDP Toolbox enables a student to maintain a so-called portfolio. The use of the Toolbox is not compulsory. The exercises can also be done on paper.

The second printing of *Managing your Competencies,* based on users' research and practical experience, has been further improved. Apart from a number of textual adaptations, a number of new subjects have been added and the description of some concepts has been refined. The number of assignments in the book has also been expanded, giving the student a choice of which ones to do.

A new section on motivation, focusing on intrinsic and extrinsic motivation, has been included. Furthermore, there is a new section on applicational and experiential learning styles. This new edition also contains new concepts such as being proactive, personal targets and the personal mission. Moreover, there is not only a new section relating to time management and the setting of priorities, but also one on the implementation of the Deming Cycle, 'plan, do, act, check' in relation to realising one's personal targets. In order to compare the higher learning courses in different countries an international set of so-called Dublin descriptors has been established. These are discussed in a separate section. Last but not least, there is a new section on competencies relating to being a member of a group.

For this revised edition we have decided not to provide a CD with all the necessary information, but to make this available on the website www.managingyourcompetencies.noordhoff.nl. This makes it possible for us to disseminate the information simply and to keep it up to date.

In this book we have often used the term 'teacher' where 'mentor', 'instructor', 'study guide' or 'coach' could also have been used. Moreover, for better readability, we consistently use 'he' where 'she' could also have been used.

Because this book is a student workbook we have not striven for a comprehensive scientific explanation of a number of definitions.

The assignments in this book were largely written by the authors. In other sections we have used the many assignments available in literature. Existing ideas and assignments have been incorporated in a modified form. In some cases we have taken over in their entirety exercises written by others.

The book *Managing your Competencies* was developed within the technical and economics departments of the Hogeschool Drenthe in Emmen. The authors have comprehensively tested the exercises in this book in conjunction with students of the aforementioned departments. We would like to thank all students who helped test the material.

We would also like to thank our colleagues at the Hogeschool Drenthe for the inspirational teaching environment. This book could not have been written without the many discussions we had with colleagues in various work groups about competency-orientated teaching. In particular, we would like to thank Jan de Geus, Gerry Geitz and Albert de Jonge for their valuable contributions to these discussions.

September 2008

Roel Grit, Emmen
Roelie Guit, Paterswolde
Nico van der Sijde, Groningen

Contents

Study Guide

Society is in a constant state of flux. New developments follow each other in rapid succession. This means you must keep on learning continually to keep your knowledge up to date. The current motto is 'A lifetime of learning'. This is why it is important in your studies to learn those things that you need to function properly in your profession, and that you keep excess baggage to an absolute minimum.

To function properly as an employee within an organisation, you must perform the required tasks of your job correctly. In other words, you must possess the correct competencies to execute your tasks properly. If you do not possess these competencies you are incompetent. Companies look for competent employees, or train existing staff to become more competent.

So what must you learn for a future profession? To establish that, you must firstly know what you can already do, what your own possibilities are, and what you will have to learn and be able to do for your future job. You will have to make up the difference between what you can do already and what you must be able to do through learning.

If you know which competencies you possess; and which competencies you want or will have to acquire for your future job, you can set up a so-called personal development plan (PDP) to achieve your goals.

Through the assignments and exercises in this book you can set up your PDP almost independently. Preferably, you will do the exercises throughout the entire period of your training course. Because the PDP is not static, you will do some exercises at the outset of your training course and others after an internship. Some assignments will have to be done more than once. This means the book is useful from the first to the last year of higher education training. Once you have correctly done the assignments, you will be fully prepared for the labour market.

Competency management takes time, but you will get full benefits from it because you will learn to work effectively. Carrying out the assignments and keeping up your personal development plan will take on average about one hour per week.

The book is arranged as follows: Chapter 1 describes what competencies are and what competency management is.
Chapter 2 provides you with assignments to further assess who you are. You will discover how others look at you, and which things are important to you. Chapter 3 teaches you where your individual qualities lie and which qualities need improving. Chapter 4 shows you how you operate within a group. Chapter 5 contains exercises and assignments to help you investigate your future labour market.

Chapter 6 differs in character. It provides you with a number of tools to help you carry out your assignments. It also serves as a reference section for now and for later, when you will be operating in the labour market.

Some assignments can be done individually, others in a group. Which assignments you should do and which you should not, is a thing best discussed with your teacher/tutor. Appendix 7 indicates which of the assignments in this book are most useful at certain points in your education, and how much time they will take.

The exercises do not have to be followed in the order given in the book. Choose those that appeal to you most at a given moment. The assignments must be executed individually, but sometimes help from your friends, family, fellow students and teachers may be necessary. They may give you valuable advice and may be capable of judging your current performance.

In order not to break up the flow of this book, we have added a number of appendices at the back. These form an essential part of the text and assignments.

The accompanying website and the PDP Toolbox
The accompanying website contains a number of check lists plus the PDP Toolbox. This software provides you among other things with tools for setting up your personality profile, a simple way of determining what you spend your time on, your personal list of activities and the competencies acquired, and also the results of the completed assignments. Of course, all the information in the Toolbox can be printed out.

Figure 0.1 depicts a couple of the Toolbox screens.

Figure 0.1 **Some PDP Toolbox screens**

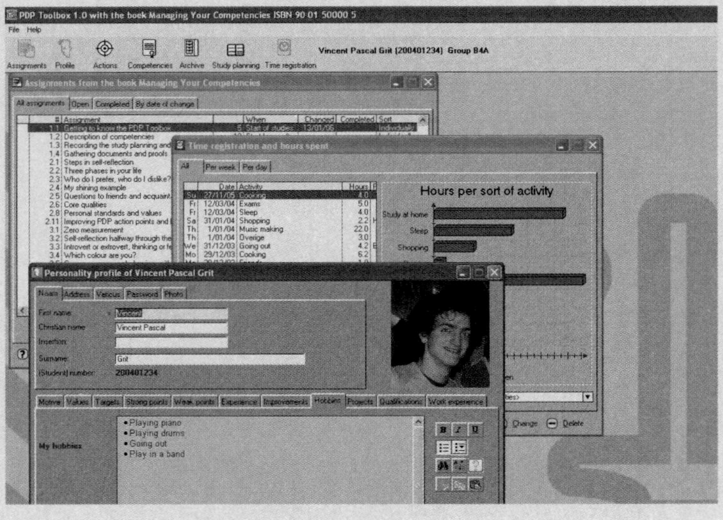

Although the use of the PDP Toolbox is not compulsory, it is strongly advised. Not only is it more enjoyable than working on paper, but it is also good for keeping everything together neatly. The advantage for your teacher is that he receives everybody's assignments and exercises in the same format, enabling him to review your PDP better and faster. It can also allow him to view your electronic PDP on his personal computer (see Appendix 1).

Note: if you do not use the Toolbox, it is imperative for you to set up a personal file in the form of a folder in which you keep the results of your completed assignments. Always be sure to keep the results of your assignments; it is very useful to compare them with earlier or later answers. If you do use the PDP Toolbox, your data will be saved automatically.

 When you see an icon like the one in the margin, it means you can use the PDP Toolbox with this exercise or assignment.

The PDP Toolbox offers the following possibilities:
· You can keep a record in it of the assignments in this book.
· You can enter your personality profile in the program with, among other things, your strong and weak points, your targets and your values and standards.
· You can also enter the competencies you already possess, and the ones you want to acquire.
· With the PDP Toolbox you can also register the marks you have obtained for exams, papers, reports and projects.
· You can enter your PDP list of action points. In fact, this is your personal development plan. With PDP action points you register what you want to work on and what your progress is.
· For the time management division, there is a help program enabling you to keep track easily of the way you spend your time.
· You can print out your data.
· By using a password, you can secure all your data.
· You will find it easy to copy your data onto a CD or diskette. You can hand this to your teacher and discuss the contents with him using the PDP Toolbox on his computer.
· You can use the Toolbox as an electronic portfolio. Traditionally, a portfolio is a file in which you store documents such as reports as proof of certain skills or competencies. Since these documents are often generated in programs such as MS Word and MS Excel, you can also use a so-called electronic portfolio. The PDP Toolbox is admirably equipped for these possibilities.

Appendix 1, 'Installing and using the PDP Toolbox', contains an explanation of how to install the PDP Toolbox.

Have fun with this book, and good luck with managing your competencies!

What is competency management?

1

In this chapter we explain what competencies are and what competency management entails. If you know what your current competencies are, and you also know which competencies you need for your training and profession in later life, you can establish which competencies you still want or need to acquire. Using a personal development plan (PDP), you can systematically work on competencies that are important to you. This chapter also informs you how you can test whether you have already acquired certain competencies. With the software program accompanying this book you can easily keep a record of the progress of your own competency management.

1.1 Competencies for your profession

What exactly is a competency? The term can be defined as follows:

> A competency is a combination of knowledge, skills, attitude and behaviour needed for proper functioning in a given professional situation.

Knowledge is what you know: for example, the theoretical part in your study books.
Skills are the things you can do: the practical application of knowledge, putting things into practice.
Attitude is about what you really want: your personal motives and preferences, that which motivates you, and which you find worth the effort.
Behaviour is your way of doing things: for example, how an advisor goes about his professional work. But it also concerns the *behavioural result*: the end results and products you provide. Of course, the latter is extremely important: to function well means producing results. Behaviour is also about how you are perceived by others.

By competencies we mean the simultaneous combination of all these aspects. They represent a combination of *knowing, ability, wanting* and *doing*.

Professional aptitude

In brief, a competency is a professional aptitude. Thus, a nurse must be able to inoculate a crying child. Without this competency he cannot function: he will be incompetent, that is, unsuitable and incompetent as a nurse.

During your training you will have to engage in competency management. What does that entail?

> Competency management is the systematic development of your personal competencies.

Someone engaged in competency management continually and systematically researches which aspects he is sufficiently competent in, and which competencies he must develop further. He not only constantly pays attention to what the profession demands of him, but also (and more importantly) how he can exploit his unique talents to the utmost. Nowadays, everybody, including you, should engage in competency management. This is because after you have completed your education you will want to have a job you like and in which you excel. You will want a job that is suitable for you. This means that throughout the course of your education you will have to work on your competencies.

In the past, this was not deemed necessary. Training was primarily focused on theoretical knowledge. Nowadays, however, companies and educational institutes are focused on competencies, so on much more than mere knowledge. This is why the modern higher education student works on integrated case studies and practical experience projects. As such, you are expected to work systematically on the development of your competencies for the full duration of your education.

Competency management is more than just passing exams. To fully and systematically develop competencies you must constantly monitor your knowledge, attitude and behaviour. Besides that, you must constantly reflect on what you know, what you can do, what you want, and what you are doing.

You can identify your inherent personality traits by answering the following questions:
1 Who am I?
2 What can I do already?
3 Where will I fit in?
4 What do I want to become?
5 What do I still have to do?

These questions will be covered in more detail in the following sections. First of all, we would like to go further into the matter of competency at the hand of an example. As we stated before, a competency is a combination of knowledge, attitude, skills and behaviour needed for **Professional situation** proper functioning in a given professional situation. A doctor, for example, must be able to persuade an overwrought and headstrong patient to rest fully and take the proper medicines. But how can he manage that? Which combination of knowledge, skills, attitude and behaviour does the doctor need to help a patient like this?

The doctor needs the following to help this patient:
· *Knowledge.* The doctor must know that certain symptoms (stress, increased heart rate, sleeplessness) point to being overwrought. He also needs to know which medicines and prescriptions are effective. He also needs to keep up with the professional literature, so that he knows about the latest medicines, therapies and so on.
· *Skills.* The doctor must be able to handle a stethoscope, for example. But he must also have communication skills:
  – He must be able to listen well and to ask pertinent questions (otherwise he cannot discover all the symptoms).
  – He must present bad news in a reassuring way: not too reassuring (because that is misleading), but not too forceful either (for that could induce panic in the patient).
  – He must be able to explain things clearly and give reasons (otherwise the headstrong patient will not believe him and consequently will not take his medicine or rest).
· *Attitude.* Every profession has its own standards and values. In this case, a caring attitude is called for. A doctor who does not think a caring attitude is important (because it is not a part of his standards and values) will not pay proper attention to his headstrong patient. Patience is also needed: a doctor must not only *be able* to listen (see skills) but he must also *want* to listen.
· *Behaviour.* In order to convince the patient the doctor must demonstrate professional behaviour and must also radiate calm and conviction. But he must also *show* his knowledge, skills and behaviour in a concrete way in order to gain a positive result.

A doctor will hopefully engage in competency management during his studies. He will constantly investigate whether he possesses enough knowledge, whether his skills are properly developed, whether his attitude (motivation, disposition, values) fits his future profession. He will also reflect on his behaviour: is my way of acting correct: am I getting enough results? This investigation is always very personal: no student has exactly the same level of knowledge, skills and attitude as his fellow students. Thus, student X may possess a lot of medical knowledge, but relatively fewer communication skills, whilst student Y possesses plenty of communication skills but relatively less medical knowledge. Student X may also be very patient, whilst Y is more impatient but also more dynamic. This means that X will have to manage his competencies differently from Y.

Description of a competency

A competency consists of:
- A result that has to be reached or the product which must be delivered
- A description of the quality of the result or product
- A professional situation in which the competency must be applied

Applying this to the competency of our doctor, the doctor must be able to persuade a completely overwrought and headstrong patient (professional situation) to rest fully and take the proper (quality) medicines (result).

The following are also examples of competencies:
- In bad weather (situation) a pilot must be able to land a plane (result) safely (quality).
- After a series of lectures (situation), a maths teacher, in using a chapter in a book, must be able to write a representative (quality) exam for a student (product).
- In building a house (situation), a bricklayer must be able to erect a wall (task) that will not fall down even under the most extreme weather conditions (quality).

1.2 Competency management: how does it work?

How should you tackle your competency management? We will now deal with the five questions to which you have to find your own answers. All those questions deal with a particular aspect of the competency and to the relationship between that competency and the future profession.

**Attitude
Personality traits**

To answer the question 'Who am I?' requires that you investigate your attitude, your personality traits and your talents. 'Attitude' is the complex of values, standards, opinions, motives, convictions, wishes and feelings. 'Motivation' is a part of your attitude. Attitude is crucial to a competency, because an unmotivated person will in general perform poorly. Therefore a doctor who does not want to be helpful or who does not want to listen will most likely not be a very good doctor, even if he possesses the necessary medical knowledge and skills.

Of course, your innate skills and personality traits also determine who you are. And your competencies are strongly influenced by your talents. That is why you have to reflect deeply on the question of whether you possess the necessary talents and qualities for a particular profession. But the question 'Who am I?' revolves mainly around what you actually do with those talents and qualities, because without motivation and the proper attitude, talents are completely useless. Of course, the talent of soccer player Ruud van Nistelrooy is innate, but his attitude is important too: he always wants to score goals, which is a good attitude for a forward. Without that attitude he would score fewer goals, despite his talent. Furthermore, he would train less intensively. Football manager Alex Ferguson obviously possesses talent befitting a coach, but his attitude is important too: his standards, values and motives centre on the view that 'everyone must strive to get the most out of himself'. Not a bad attitude for a coach!

The question 'Who am I?' therefore relates to talents but mainly attitude and motivational traits. You can discover who you are by doing the assignments, sometimes helped by people in your environment, such as friends, relatives or fellow students. Of course, a lot will be familiar to you already, but other things may be new to you. In any case, it is useful to investigate to what extent your attitude and personality traits are suited to the professional competencies needed. A soccer player must utilise his talent by training hard, but first he has to discover that he has that talent. A shy student who wants to become a salesperson must compensate for his shyness, but he must first recognise that shyness in himself.

Knowledge
Skills

To answer the question 'What can I do already?' requires that you investigate your knowledge and skills. Do you already possess enough of the knowledge needed for certain professional situations? Do you know enough? And how about your skills? What are your strongest points? What are your weaker points? Remember: skills without knowledge lack depth, and knowledge not coupled with skills has insufficient practical value. It is the combination that really matters.

Kind of profession

Of course, the question of 'Where do I fit in?' is directly linked to the previous question. But this question mainly relates to the kind of profession you are attracted to, and not concrete professions per se. Therefore, it concerns the criteria your future profession has to meet, or as you see it, as well as in which situation you will work most efficiently. A 'practical man' will not want a profession in which he is formulating policies behind his desk: he wants to tackle things. One person functions well in a purely formal and businesslike work environment, another in an informal, 'friendly' work environment. One person requires strong leadership and clear-cut assignments, whilst another needs freedom and creativity.

Professions

To answer the question 'What do I want to become?' requires that you investigate which professions are most suited to your attitude, knowledge and skills. Making choices can be difficult, especially if you do not know what there is to choose from. This book and the exercises in it will help you to make these choices so that later you find a suitable profession, a profession that ties in with your competencies. This is why the question 'What do I want to become?' is important for your competency management.

Points for improvement

To answer the question 'What do I still have to do?' requires that you investigate what needs improving – your points for improvement – especially in relation to your knowledge and skills. In addressing the question 'What can I do already?' you investigated your strong and weak points. The weak points need to be improved, especially if they are required for your future profession. Some assigments contain instructions for formulating study targets. These primarily relate to knowledge and skills because 'attitude' is more difficult to change.

Personal Development Plan

You will have to deal with these five questions all through your training. In fact, in this way you will make a PDP, a personal development plan, for the full course of your studies. You begin with it in your first year, and in the final year you will have completed your PDP.

Let us now talk about your studies: once you have a job, you will often be working on a different PDP. Many companies and institutions encourage this. To reiterate, the PDP is your plan. The P of 'personal' is very important. In your studies you lay down the foundation for your career and life. For a company, a diploma and list of results are not sufficient. Those in charge will want to know who you are, what you can do, and if you fit in with them. They will want to get to know the individual behind the diploma. Of course, the goal of your studies is fixed. The course itself will determine which competencies must be attained for the final exams. But you yourself determine its individual content. You decide how to attain those competencies, and you decide which parts of it suit you best. You are the one who personalises your diploma.

Personality profile

With the PDP you set up your own personality profile. You will do that for your studies, for your future sphere of employment, but most of all for yourself. You are not on your own. This book will help you with it through assignments, your teachers will assist you with the assignments, and so on.

1.3   Testing your competencies

As you complete the assignments in this book, your PDP will be tested, and at regular intervals. In fact, all the assignments are small tests. You should view these tests as instruments, as a means to progress. Without this type of instrument you would have no grip on your PDP. With the assignments you continually record where you are in your personal development, and you do this for your teachers though mainly for yourself. You will also record on a continual basis what remains to be done. What you will be doing is essentially engaging in competency management.

You will test the progress of your competencies in various ways:
- *By reflection.* You think about your strong and weak points, and about your standards and values.
- *Through tests.* You will do a number of tests – this book contains a fair number of them – that give you an impression of your competencies, and you will analyse what the test results mean for your competency management.
- *Through feedback.* You will listen to the opinion of others about your performance (i.e. your competencies), and you will consider what those opinions mean for your competency management.
- *Through research.* You will investigate which competencies are important to your future sphere of employment and whether they suit you or not.

We have previously stated that behaviour is also a determining factor in your competencies: your professional performance, but especially the results you attain. Anyone who does not come up with results is obviously incompetent. That is why getting results is part of the process of testing your competencies. The results will later count as pieces of evidence and may include test results as well as products (which includes research papers), testimonials, assessments by fellow students and test results. Part of competency management is the gathering of pieces of evidence and updating the results to show others what your strong points are. A handy way of doing this is by means of your portfolio (see the following section).

1.4   The PDP Toolbox as electronic portfolio

Portfolio

The folder in which an artist keeps his works is called a portfolio. He uses it to show others what he has done: his portfolio contains evidence of his abilities. The portfolio of paintings shows he is a competent painter (depending, of course, on whether the paintings are actually any good). The term 'portfolio' was transferred to education from the art and advertising world; with a portfolio a student can prove what he 'can do'. As a student you will have to keep all sorts of documents as proof of attaining certain competencies. You will have to assemble your own portfolio showing what you can do and what you have attained so far. The portfolio will also contain feedback from fellow students and a description of your study goals: it will therefore also reflect your development and what you still have to do in order to develop further.

Electronic portfolio

A portfolio can be a real folder with papers, reports, minutes testimonials, written assessments by fellow students or teachers and so on. But it is also possible to use an electronic portfolio. After all, you will often generate documents in programs such as MS Word and MS Excel.

The PDP Toolbox enables you – through the Archive section – to store your electronic documents in an orderly fashion on your hard drive. You can simply select files you want to save in the Toolbox from the program.

Assignment 1.1 Introducing the PDP Toolbox

In this assignment you will become acquainted with the program PDP Toolbox, which is on the website accompanying this book. You can use it to record everything related to your PDP Toolbox. In the study guide and Appendix 1 you will find information about installing and working with the PDP Toolbox.

a Read Appendix 1 carefully. Install the PDP Toolbox according to the instructions in the appendix. After installing it, check the various functions of the program.

b Go to the Personality Profile section and enter:
- Your personal data
- Your preparatory training
- Your hobbies and interests
- Your part-time job(s) (if any)

Assignment 1.2 Description of competencies

a Study Section 1.2 and describe three competencies of a profession fitting your education.

b For every competency state under point *a* which knowledge, skill and attitude you must have in order to acquire this competency. Also indicate which results must be attained.

c Study Section 1.2 and describe three competencies you will attain through your training.

d For every competency state under point *c* which knowledge, skills and attitude you must have for acquiring the competency.

Make a report of this assignment in your PDP Toolbox in the Assignments section.

Assignment 1.3 Which competencies will you need to have mastered within the near future?

a Describe the competencies which are crucial to the next few months of your education.

b Indicate what you will have to know, what you can do and must do. Also indicate the appropriate attitude for that.

c Indicate how you (or your project group) are going to tackle this.

Write a report on this assignment in your PDP Toolbox in the Assignments section.

Assignment 1.4 Recording your study timetabling and assessments

During your training, teachers will assess your results, for example, by means of exams and papers. You will find it easy to plan exams and the like in your PDP Toolbox and record the results. The following assignments are best done quarterly or mid-term.

a Make a schedule of the exams and so on that you want to complete in your current year or term. Enter your schedule in the study planning section of the PDP Toolbox.

b Afterwards, enter your results in the PDP Toolbox.

Assignment 1.5 Gathering documents and evidence

During your studies you will write papers, reports and so on in programs such as MS Word and MS Excel. Often you will want to or will be required to save these documents. The PDP Toolbox enables you – through the Archive section – to store all your electronic documents systematically on your hard drive. From the Toolbox you can simply select a file that you want to save. After that a copy of the file will be saved with the other data in your PDP Toolbox.

Gather the important electronic documents you have produced so far and save them with the Toolbox.

Who am I?

2

In the first chapter we explained that a competency not only consists of knowledge and skills, but also of personality traits and attitude. For competency management this means that the question 'Who am I?' is important. This is why in this chapter you will investigate who you are through self-analysis. A number of exercises and tests will help you to get to know yourself better. Enter the results in your personal file, or better still, enter them in your PDP Toolbox. Through self-reflection and the receiving of feedback you will discover your good and bad qualities. Next you will investigate which core qualities you possess. The Enneagram method will help you determine which basic type of human being you are. Then you will start looking at your personal standards and values. By means of the learning styles test and the Kolb learning cycle, you will determine the best learning method for you. The assignments concerning applicational and experiential learning styles will help you work on your active study attitude. At the end of this chapter you will start to set up your personal development plan on the basis of your assignment results in your PDP Toolbox. In this plan you will record which competencies you want to attain and which activities you will carry out to achieve this level.

2.1   Why self-analysis?

Imagine that you want to build your own home. You buy a plot of land for a considerable sum. You buy expensive bricks but start working without a proper floor plan. You put all your energy into erecting a wall. Whistling while you work, you build a wall, and then another. Then you notice you have forgotten the windows, so you hack a piece out of your newly built wall and place a window in it. A bit further on, you hack out another piece for the door you forgot. Then the walls start subsiding because you forgot the foundations. Strange? Of course it is: nobody builds a house in this way.

Yet many people take a similar approach to their life and career. They work hard without knowing why they do it and where they will end up. If you want to get the most out of your life, you will have to know what your goal is. You will also have to know what suits you best. In a manner of speaking, you will have to make a sort of floor plan for your life and career.

To find out what you want to do with your life and career, you will have to find out who you are. What would you like best and what absolutely not; what is important to you, what are you good at and which aspects can be improved? This you will find out by means of self-analysis.

Once you have completed this chapter, you will see more clearly who you are, which qualities you possess and what your goals are. You will have laid a solid foundation upon which to build up and direct your life and career. You will be in no doubt about the qualities and skills you already possess and which qualities you will need to develop in **Personal** the times ahead. You can record all your findings in your personal **development plan** development plan. This plan helps you to keep track of your progress and allows you to effectively manage your personal development.

2.2   Self-reflection

Reflection is the bouncing back of light in a mirror. You can see yourself in a mirror. Self-reflection is holding a mirror up to yourself to see who you are and what you are doing. You reflect on your actions, on all the things you do or fail to do, and you closely investigate your personality traits and your attitude. You keep asking yourself questions like: what kind of person am I, what sort of behaviour do I approve of, which talents do I possess? Is my behaviour appropriate to the situation? Once you have a good insight into these aspects, you can work more effectively on your personal and professional development. As such reflection is the basis of competency management. But reflection is not something you pick up in a day: you can only learn it through repetition.

The reflection process occurs in the following steps (see also Figure 2.1):

Reflection steps plan

Step 1   *Gaining practical experience*
Step 2   *Looking back and overseeing*
  · What happened? What went well and what went wrong?
  · Did I demonstrate a professional attitude?
  · How better to approach it?
Step 3   *Determining a strategy*
  · Why am I tackling it and how do I go about it?
  · What is my objective?
  · What should I pay attention to?
  · What do I want to try?
Step 4   *Gaining practical experience*
Step 5   *Analysing*
  · What happened?
  · What was important?
  · What was the key to the problem?
Step 6   *Determining a new strategy*
  · How could I approach it more efficiently?

And so on

Figure 2.1 **Steps in self-reflection**

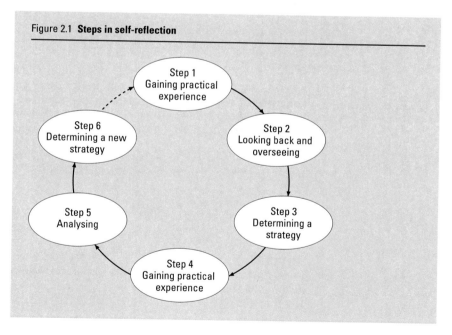

Imagine that for the first time in your studies you are to give a
presentation to your group about a certain subject. You have never
given a presentation before, and are fairly intimidated. Giving a
presentation is the practical experience referred to in Step 1 of
Figure 2.1. Afterwards you are not satisfied with your presentation and
you try to determine what went right and what went wrong (Step 2).

Then you think of a strategy to perform better next time. For example, you could read a book about giving presentations. You could also decide that for your next presentation you will first practice in front of a mirror to see if the presentation is not too long (Step 3). Because you want to learn how to give a better presentation, you arrange to give another presentation as soon as possible (Step 4). After this additional practical experience you follow Steps 5 and 6: you analyse your second presentation and determine a new strategy. After that you go through the cycle in Figure 2.1 again.

The trick is first to gain practical experience, to analyse it and devise a strategy for the next practical experience, then gain more practical experience, analyse it again, and so on. Going about things like this means that you will really learn from experience and constantly improve yourself. That self-improvement is, of course, a part of competency management.

Assignment 2.1 Steps in self-reflection
Draw up a plan of steps for the following tasks. Do this according to Figure 2.1 and the example given for it.
- Chairing a meeting
- Writing a report or minutes.

 Make a report of this assignment in your PDP Toolbox in the Assignments section.

A number of assignments that will help you make a thorough self-analysis are given here. The first four assignments are good assignments to start with. Assignment 2.6 requires you to have gained experience in reflection. For assignment 2.7 it is important for you to have worked in a project group or in a team for some time.

In doing the assignments receiving feedback and reflection is important, and so are the rules relating to them.

Your life is influenced by various incidents. Some incidents may be so dramatic that your life will never be the same afterwards. A child that has been bullied a lot at school may, as a result, suffer severely in later life. He may still be afraid of being hurt, and possibly may not always open up to other people. On the other hand, someone who was often complimented as a child will have a lot of self-confidence later on. If you have finished your studies after much hard work you will have demonstrated to yourself and to others that you possess a lot of perseverance.

It is good to reflect on which events have had an impact on your life. Those events have made you what you are today. Events shape you and contribute to your development. Gaining insight in to why you approach life the way you do means that you can change it.

Assignment 2.2 Three phases of your life

a Divide your life into three time stages (see Table 2.1) and describe what was the most important event for you in each stage.

Table 2.1 **Three phases in your life**

Phase	Important event	Which positive influence did this event have?	Which negative influence did this event have?
0 – 10 years			
10 – 18 years			
18 – 25 years			

b Now answer the following questions:
- Why were these events particularly important to you?
- What influence did they have on the rest of your life?
- What have you learned from these events?
- What do these events say about your character, i.e., about your personality traits?
- What will you do with these insights?

 Make a report of this assignment in your PDP Toolbox in the Assignments section.

Everybody has a mix of good and bad characteristics, but not everyone knows his own particular characteristics. It is difficult to view oneself objectively. A handy tool for getting to know your own characteristics is given in Assignment 2.3. Once it is clear to you what your positive and negative characteristics are you will know what you will have to work on in the times ahead.

Assignment 2.3 Who do I like, who do I dislike?

With some people you get along, with others you definitely do not. You like some people a lot and others you dislike. Try finding out why you prefer some people and why others turn you off. The way in which you judge people says something about yourself as well.

a Who do I dislike?
Think of a person you do not like at all. You can choose more than one person.
- Write down as many negative traits of this person as possible.
- Which of these negative traits do you possess yourself?

b Who do I like?
Think of a person you really like. You can choose a number of people.
- Write down as many positive traits of this person as possible.
- Which of these positive traits do you possess yourself?

Table 2.2 will help you on your way.

Table 2.2 **Negative and positive traits**

Negative traits in others	Positive traits in others	Negative traits in myself	Positive traits in myself
• Likes to gossip	• Helpful	• Lazy	• Ambitious
• Demotivating	• Cheerful	• Not very flexible	• Hard-working
• Demands a lot of attention	• Hard-working	• Bad listener	• Good negotiator
• Lazy	• Ambitious	• Bad planner	• Loyal
• ...	• ...	• ...	• ...
• ...	• ...	• ...	• ...

 Make a report of this assignment in your PDP Toolbox in the Assignments section.

Assignment 2.4 My big role model

Often somebody has a big role model, someone who has had a major influence on his life. It may be a remote idol, but equally it could be someone nearby, such as a history teacher who has instilled a love of history in him, or a neighbour who has built up a flourishing business out of nothing.

Think of someone that you know well (a parent, a member of the family, a teacher, a friend) and who has a big influence on your life, someone you respect and admire.
- In what respects did he or she influence you?
- How did he or she influence you?
- What were his or her strong points?
- What were his or her weak points?
- What would you like to attain that that person has attained?
- How do you imagine you will realise that?

 Make a report of this assignment in your PDP Toolbox in the Assignments section.

2.3   Receiving feedback

Self-reflection means that you hold up a mirror to yourself; in giving feedback someone else holds the mirror up for you. In order to make a proper self-analysis you need the input of other people, such as family, friends or fellow students. They look at you differently than you do yourself and may be able to tell you things you were not aware of. Feedback is the giving of comments on your behaviour by others. By asking for feedback you open yourself to learning from everyday practice and modifying your behaviour if you think you need to.

In asking for feedback, remember the following rules:
- Do not start to argue or to defend yourself.
- Be open to the feedback given.

- Try to understand the feedback.
- Listen attentively and ask for clarification if needed.
- Show your appreciation to the person giving the feedback.
- Judge the feedback for its usefulness. What can you do with it?
- Do something with the feedback.
- Do not take criticism as an attack on your person.
- Be open to compliments; do not pretend they are unimportant.

Some questions you could ask during a feedback session could include the following:
- What went right?
- What can be improved?
- What could be done differently?

In Sections 6.3 and 6.4 fuller attention is given to the exchanging of feedback in groups.

Assignment 2.5 Questions to put to friends and acquaintances
If all went well with earlier exercises, you will have established an image of yourself. The question is now whether others see you in the same way as you do yourself. Maybe you think others like you, while they may think you are conceited and not very nice. You could have a completely wrong image of yourself. With this assignment you will find out if your self-image is correct.

a Choose three people from your environment and ask them the following three questions:
   1 What should I definitely continue doing?
   2 What should I immediately stop doing?
   3 What should I change immediately?

Table 2.3 shows what kind of answers a mother, friend or fellow student might give.

Table 2.3 **How do others see me?**

What should I definitely continue doing?	What should I immediately stop doing?	What should I change immediately?
Mother: *be caring towards fellow human beings* Friend: *play soccer, be sportsmanlike* Fellow student: *write college reports*	Mother: *smoking* Friend: *making corny jokes* Fellow student: *doubting that you can handle your studies*	Mother: *bring order to the chaos in your room* Friend: *make holiday plans in advance* Fellow student: *arrive on time*

b After the questionnaire has been filled in by the people you chose, analyse the list.
   - Are there any unexpected responses?
   - Did you expect these answers? Explain.

- Were you aware that they appreciated these qualities in you in particular?
- Were you aware that they were irritated by certain things? Do you plan to change these? Why will you, why won't you?
- Will you act on the advice of these people? Why will you, why won't you?

 Make a report of this assignment in your PDP Toolbox in the Assignments section.

2.4   Core qualities

Positive trait
Daniel Ofman

A core quality is a positive trait you possess. Researcher Daniel Ofman (2002) defines this as follows:

> Core qualities are characteristics or personal traits that belong to the essence or core of a person. They pervade the entire being ... the quality colours the human being; it is the specific strength you immediately associate with him or her.

Some examples of core qualities are flexibility, thoughtfulness, empathy, independence, being sympathetic, and analytical perspicacity. These are the traits or personal characteristics others appreciate in you but that you probably find normal yourself. So normal, in fact, that you do not even notice them any more. Everyone's core qualities differ. People are usually able to identify three main core qualities.

If you know what your core qualities are, you can simply find out your weak points by filling in Ofman's core quadrant model. This model is represented diagrammatically in Figure 2.2.

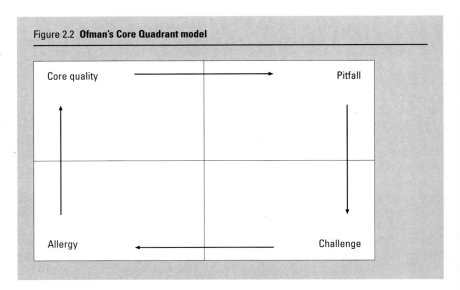

Figure 2.2 **Ofman's Core Quadrant model**

Core quality   Pitfall

Allergy   Challenge

Pitfall

A pitfall is the negative side of a core quality: the core quality has been taken too far. The pitfall is not the opposite of the core quality, but a surplus of the core quality. If, for example, your core quality is having a caring attitude, there is a chance that this quality will be taken too far, to condescension. Condescension towards others represents your pitfall and you must be careful not to fall into it. If responsibility is your core quality (to take another example), there is a chance that it will be taken too far and become interfering behaviour (because you feel responsible for the work of others), or of becoming stressed (because you want to do things too well). These represent pitfalls too.

Challenge

The challenge is the positive opposite of the pitfall. For example, if listening attentively is your core quality and the attendant pitfall is passivity, then your challenge is to speak your mind more clearly.

Allergy

An allergy is a negative reaction on your part to someone who represents your challenge. Your challenge is something that will always trouble you. If others ask too much of it you will become stressed and irritated. For example, if it is your challenge to speak your mind more clearly, you can be desperately irritated if someone dominates you and does not listen to you. An allergy is the opposite of your core quality. If you were to notice the allergic quality within yourself you would be appalled.

Figure 2.3 gives an example of a completed core quadrant for the core quality 'independence'.

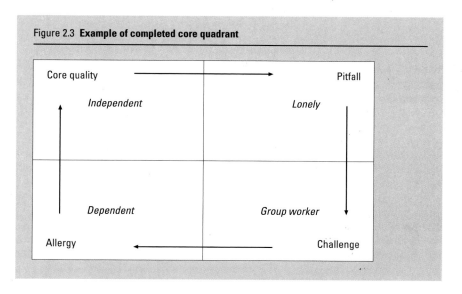

Figure 2.3 **Example of completed core quadrant**

If your core quality is 'independence' you will prefer to do everything on your own. You probably feel that you work faster and more efficiently on your own. Your pitfall is that you literally do everything by yourself, that you engage in solo performances and to the extent become lonely. Your challenge is found in teamwork; that means you will have to learn how to work together with other people. This is a nuisance to someone who prefers to work on his own. If you have to cooperate with someone in the group with a dependent disposition, there is a good chance that conflicts will arise between you and that person. That person is too representative of your challenge. So you have an allergic reaction to him.

The core quadrant is a tool to help you develop. A core quadrant gives you insight into your personality traits, your strong and your weak points. It also teaches you that your weak points arise from your strong points. That makes it easier to work on those points. On top of that, the core quadrant gives you insight into your behaviour and its backgrounds. This makes you realise faster why you have problems dealing with particular situations. Then you can decide to do something about it. Core qualities are not static. As you continue to develop, your core qualities will continue to develop as well. If you work on them according to a plan, you will be engaged in managing your competencies.

Assignment 2.6 Core qualities

a On the basis of Figure 2.3 make three empty core quadrants and in each enter a core quality that you feel fits you. Most people have difficulty saying something positive about themselves. If this applies to you, try starting by entering the allergy. Most of the time you can easily identify what irritates you in someone else. Or you can ask people in your environment what irritates them about you and start entering the answers under your pitfall.

b By watching, observing and reflecting you will gain a good insight into your qualities and behaviour.
Write down three concrete practical experiences:
1 In which situation did your core quality come out best?
2 In which situation was there too great an arousal of one of your challenges?
3 In which situation did you demonstrate an allergic reaction?

c On the basis of the assignment above decide if you want to change something in your behaviour.
  · Describe what you want to change
  · Why you want to change it
  · How you think to make the change

 Make a report of this assignment in your PDP Toolbox in the Assignments section.

2.5   Enneagram

Core qualities relate to elements of your behaviour which you see as positive. In Section 2.4 you learned that you take things too far ending up in a pitfall. In the Enneagram these matters are considered further. The Enneagram is based upon an experience theory according to which people are divided into nine basic types (*ennea* is the Greek word for 'nine'). According to this theory a person belongs to one of nine basic types. These types are often indicated by a number. For example, we speak about 'the One' for the basic type perfectionist, and about 'the Two' for the helper type. Figure 2.4 shows the basic types described by the Enneagram.

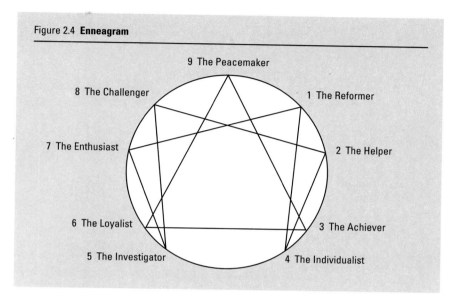

Figure 2.4 **Enneagram**

The lines in the diagram have a deeper meaning which we will not enter into here. Knowledge of the basic types can help you to know and understand yourself and others better. You will become more conscious of your own behaviour, and also of your personality traits. You will come to see that the irritating behaviour of others is not intentionally meant to hurt you. By working with an Enneagram, you will learn to look at yourself and others with a certain distance.

We shall now give a short description of each type and the accompanying characteristic professions.

The One: The Reformer
Reformers are realistic and principled. The One tries to realise his high ideals. Ones often think things can always be improved, and they are not easily satisfied. Reformers can become frustrated because life and people are not exactly the way they should be according to their expectations. They can be disappointed in their own imperfections and also in not being able to come up to their own high standards. Characteristic professions: politician, teacher, police officer, minister.

The Two: The Helper
Helpers are warm, involved, caring and sensitive to other people's needs. They understand others and offer help to their fellow human beings. The underlying goal of the helper is to show his own

superiority compared to others. Often this is an unconscious goal of the Two.
Characteristic professions: nurse, social worker (care sector).

The Three: The Achiever

Achievers work hard, are optimistic, energetic, self-assured and purposeful. Threes forego everything to attain success, if needs be at the cost of others. Achievers can be very pushy.
Characteristic professions: manager, salesperson, designer, something in the media or advertising world.

The Four: The Individualist

Individualists are sensitive, warm and self-aware. A Four feels he is unique and wants others to think so too. Individualists get their energy from others and are constantly wondering 'What do you think of me?' They are very instinctive (intuitive) and introverted, sometimes melancholy. Fours often feel they are not understood.
Characteristic professions: novelist, artist, actor or musician (artistic professions).

The Five: The Investigator

Investigators have a need for knowledge and gather as much knowledge as possible. They are inquisitive, analytical, persevering and sensitive. In many situations they often have problems dealing with their emotions, because essentially they are sensitive people. Their thinking and feelings do not run parallel, and this is why they often come across as level-headed and businesslike.
Characteristic professions: researcher, inspector, librarian or technician.

The Six: The Loyalist

Loyalists have a sense of responsibility, are trustworthy and attach importance to being loyal towards family, friends, groups and authorities. The Six attaches importance to tradition and is a good team worker.
Characteristic professions: solicitor, public prosecutor or detective.

The Seven: The Enthusiast

Enthusiasts are lively, energetic and optimistic. The enthusiast is spontaneous and imaginative and wants to contribute his bit to the world. The Seven is impulsive and naive and is ambivalent about entering relationships. Sevens are extremely persuasive.
Characteristic professions: preferably various jobs simultaneously or independent professions.

The Eight: The Challenger

Challengers go 'straight to it' and are independent, self-assured and protective. They come across as strong personalities, often taking charge and exposing injustice. Challengers have an attitude of 'I will not be taken advantage of' and want to keep control over the situation. This is why the Eight wants to be informed about everything. He is often possessive.
Characteristic professions: manager and director (executive functions).

The Nine: The Peacemaker

Peacemakers strive for harmony with their fellow human beings. Nines believe in the goodness of man, are supportive and can put things in perspective. Peacemakers are impartial judges, have an understanding of others, but can be indolent. They shy away from and avoid difficult situations and do not count on others being interested in their problems.

Characteristic professions: a profession in which they do not have to take the initiative and in which there is little stressful or conflictual behaviour.

Fixations

All basic types of the Enneagram can suffer from so-called fixations. By fixations we mean that one is continually focused on certain things and thoughts, one is 'attached' to them, as it were, without noticing it. Fixations have a positive and a negative side. The positive **Seduction** side could be described as seduction and the negative side could be **Avoidance** described as avoidance. For example, as a child you have developed behaviour ensuring love and attention, and that behaviour is still yours, as it has proven successful. This is the positive fixation. The reverse also occurs: you avoid behaviour that causes pain. You experience pain by unsuccessful behaviour, i.e. behaviour that was **Blockade** not appreciated. Furthermore, every type has its own blockade: behaviour that leads to making the same mistake again and again. Table 2.4 'Enneagram basic types' lists which blockades belong to each basic type.

Assignment 2.7 Enneagram

a Study the nine types of the Enneagram in this Section and in Table 2.4 'Enneagram basic types'.
  Which type or types are you? Give your reasons.

b Use a search engine on the Internet to find an Enneagram test. For example, type in the search words 'Enneagram' and 'test' (during the writing of this book an extended test could be found on www.enneagraminstitute.com).
  Take the test and discover which basic type you are according to the test.
  Do you recognise yourself in that type? Describe two concrete examples showing you are that type.

c On the basis of assignments a and b decide if you want to change something in your behaviour.
  - What do you want to change?
  - Why do you want to change that?
  - How are you going to change that?

 Make a report of this assignment in your PDP Toolbox in the Assignments section.

Table 2.4 Enneagram basic types

Type	Fixation	Blockade	Challenge
The One The Reformer 'I am right'	• Tempted by: perfectionism • Likes to avoid: imperfection • People with anger as passions are motivated by it. It gives them power, until the lid blows off.	Anger	Patience, acceptance of the imperfect
The Two: The Helper 'I help'	• Tempted by: social superiority • Likes to avoid: need • People with this passion feel superior. They like to be seen as being important to other people's lives	Pride	True solidarity
The Three: The Achiever 'I am successful'	• Tempted by: success • Likes to avoid: failure • Self-deceit is coupled with vanity. Threes create an image of themselves as they would like to appear in other people's eyes. They live according to an image of what they would like to be, and this image is unrealistic	Vanity	Sincerity, honesty
The Four: The Individualist 'I am different'	• Tempted by: beauty • Likes to avoid: inferiority • Fours feel that no one understands them. They are not envious of material wellbeing but of happiness: why he and why not me?	Envy	Balanced feelings
The Five: The Investigator 'I understand'	• Tempted by: wisdom • Likes to avoid: emptiness • People with this passion need time, space and certain things for themselves and do not like to share these with other people. They are collectors of knowledge.	Greed	Objectivity, ability to put things in perspective
The Six: The Loyalist 'I do my duty'	• Tempted by: certainty • Likes to avoid: doubt • Sixes look for security and protection by those in authority, but fear those things at the same time. Sixes continually have 'Yes' and 'No' in their heads: I am loyal towards authority or oppose it.	Fear, recklessness	Courage
The Seven: The Enthusiast 'I am happy'	• Tempted by: pleasure • Likes to avoid: pain • People with this passion search relentlessly for pleasure. They lack moderation and go from one pleasurable event to the next.	Gluttony, more is always better	Sober-mindedness
The Eight: The Challenger 'I am strong'	• Tempted by: power • Likes to avoid: powerlessness • People with this fixation want to keep control over the situation and use power to do that.	Appetite, must have what I want	Innocence, accepting the vulnerable child in oneself
The Nine: The Peacemaker 'I am satisfied'	• Tempted by: delicacy • Likes to avoid: conflict • Nines do not get upset and tend to let all things slide by.	Sloth and laziness	Decisiveness, taking responsibility

2.6   Values and motives

In Chapter 1 we explained that attitude – including standards and values – forms a part of competencies. For example, a salesperson oblivious to 'client friendliness' is a bad salesperson. In reflecting on your own competencies you should also reflect on your standards and values.

Motives

Everyone has within himself a sense of what standards and values are. Older people and politicians often speak of a lack of standards and values, which is causing society to 'degenerate'. Values are therefore closely connected with standards relating to what you are allowed to do or ought not to do. But most of all they are things viewed as worth pursuing. In that sense, values are also motives. Someone who values customer-friendliness will pursue being customer-friendly in his job. Someone who considers respect an important value will strive to respect others and will expect others to respect him. Of course, we all have different values and motives. One person will find it normal to jump a red traffic light or to be late for school. Others will not. One person may find results important; another, having a good time with friends.

Some examples of values and motives
- Fame (being recognised by as many people as possible in the street)
- Ambition (the feeling of performing well, accomplishing something, craftsmanship)
- Adventure (new and challenging experiences)
- Promotion (striving to rise rapidly in an organisation)
- Variation (wanting to do many different things)
- Excelling (the will to win; wanting to be able to fight for a just cause)
- Affection (love, warmth)
- Family happiness (presumes leisure time)
- Friendship (presumes leisure time as well)
- Creativity (wanting to be imaginative; wanting to be able to develop a lot of original ideas)
- Practically oriented (wanting to execute concrete assignments with concrete results; finding it important to make tangible products)
- Economic security (a steady job, no risks)
- Freedom (wanting to make your own decisions)
- Cooperation (working together with other people, having good relationships with colleagues; engaging in team efforts)
- Self-respect (the feeling of pride in oneself)
- Sense of duty (doing something for your country, your work)
- Efficiency: attaining good results as quickly as possible
- Optimalism: getting the most out of things no matter how much time it takes
- Wealth (for example, being able to buy everything you like)
- Sense of responsibility
- Power (being recognised as an authority; you determine what is going to happen; having influence on others)
- Recognition (wanting to hear from others that you are good at your job or in another field; status)

- Honesty and sincerity
- Stability (order and peace in your own life; a good balance between work and private life)
- Leisure (among other things, wanting to have enough free time to be able to do your own things)
- Self-realisation (wanting to grow personally; an increase in knowledge and skills; getting the utmost out of yourself)
- Commitment (wanting to do something for society, possibly deriving from your belief system)
- Health (for example, not a job with a lot of unhealthy stress)

Assignment 2.8 Personal values and motives

a In the list above, we described a number of different values. Study the list and see if you can add a number of other values. From this new list make a Top Ten of the most important values to you.

b If in doing this assignment you are working in a small group, discuss the different results with each other. If necessary, adjust your own Top Ten.

c Your values and motives may differ from what society, your educational background, your family – in brief, your environment – considers normal. Maybe you think it is normal to arrive too late or to drive through a stop signal. Investigate yourself to find out which values and motives you have that are not subscribed to by others.

d Which deviating motives that others have irritate you?

e Designate a number of values and motives relating to the execution of your future profession.

 On the basis of this assignment make a report of your own standards and values in your PDP Toolbox in the Personal Profile section, under the heading 'Values'.

2.7 Motivation

Intrinsic and extrinsic motivation

When you are motivated to do something, your performance will be better. You will enjoy the things that you do. There are two kinds of motivation: intrinsic and extrinsic motivation. When you are motivated intrinsically you will work hard because of your idea that you can accomplish something that will satisfy you. That is directly related to your values and motives (see preceding section). With extrinsic motivation you will work hard because there is a reward at the end of the assignment: a good test result, for example. People who are motivated intrinsically have fewer problems maintaining their motivation. They are less easily distracted by extraneous matters.

We assume you started your studies fully motivated. In the next assignment you will write down where your motivation for doing the study course lies. If you can see clearly why you are passionate about the studies you are following you will be able to build up your motivation again if you enter a rough patch during the course of your studies.

Assignment 2.9 Where does my motivation come from?

Finish the following sentence. More than one answer is possible.

I chose this course because
- I want to help others.
- I want to influence others.
- I want to help others solve problems.
- I want to be an efficient team worker.
- I want to learn to communicate clearly.
- I want to be able to empathize with others.
- I want to train and educate people.
- I want to learn how to sell services or goods.
- I want to learn how to resolve conflicts.
- I want to think up and develop new ideas.
- I want to set up and/or execute policies.
- I want to have a financial understanding.
- I ....
- I ....

Now you have stated in a few sentences why you have chosen this course.

Write a report on this assignment in your PDP Toolbox in the section 'Assignments'. If you hit a temporary low during your studies you can always refer to this report on why you chose this particular course of education. This will help you to focus again and build up your motivation.

2.8 Learning styles and Kolb's Learning Cycle

Suppose that as a birthday gift you get a digital watch with lots of little buttons to correctly set the time for the watch and find out all its functions. You can use various strategies for correctly setting the time on the watch and finding out all its functions. You could begin by consulting the manual. Or you could experiment long enough for you to understand how the watch works. You could also try to remember how you set the time on a digital alarm clock you bought in the past and use this experience to set your watch. Finally, you could ask someone who owns a similar watch to explain to you how the device works. Ultimately and whatever approach you used you will have learned how the watch works. Clearly, learning something can occur in various ways.

The society in which we live is constantly changing due to the many developments (including technological ones) it is undergoing. But not everyone learns in the same way: as the example shows. There are different ways of learning (styles of learning). To be able to learn efficiently, it is important to know something about how learning happens and what style of learning suits you best. You can adjust your way of studying accordingly. You can learn, for example, by acquiring a theoretical clarity about a problem before you go ahead and tackle it. Or you may want to practice and take a practical approach. Learning, of course, has everything to do with the development of your competencies, because the more efficiently you learn, the more competent you will become. This is why it is important to find out which style of learning is most effective for you.

David Kolb

Learning cycle

To be able to learn and study well you need a number of skills. David Kolb (1998) distinguishes four phases in the learning process, which he has represented in his so-called learning cycle (see Figure 2.5). Each phase requires different skills.

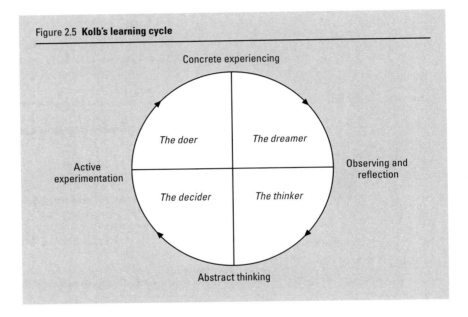

Figure 2.5 **Kolb's learning cycle**

Four learning phases

According to Kolb learning consists of four learning phases:
1 *Concrete experiencing.* This is gaining experience by personally undergoing something. For example, you could write your first report for your course.
2 *Observing and reflection.* On the basis of a concrete experience reflection takes place. You look back at what went right and what went wrong. Your report was rejected; you have to do it again. You try to determine what went wrong and what went right.
3 *Abstract thinking.* You gather your observations and translate them into a theory. You start to wonder when a report is 'right'. You decide – also based on a suitable book – that a good report must contain an introduction, a summary and a conclusion.
4 *Active experimentation.* Based on your theory you set up new hypotheses, or you deduce new plans and ideas. You are going to experiment with these in practice. You sit behind your PC and improve the report based on the results of the above step. This time

you *do* include an introduction, summary and conclusion and hand in the report for a new assessment.

Kolb sees learning as a cyclical process. In an efficient and active way of studying you go through all four learning phases of the learning cycle. Depending on your style of learning (see later) you will have a preference for a particular point in the learning cycle.

Four styles of learning

Everyone has his own preferred style of learning. Once you know what your preferred style of learning is, you can develop more efficiently. Kolb distinguishes four styles of learning that arise out of a combination of two of the four phases in the learning cycle:
1 The dreamer: concrete experiencing/observing and reflection
2 The thinker: observing and reflection/abstract thinking
3 The decider: abstract thinking/actively experimenting
4 The doer: actively experimenting/concrete experiencing

The characteristics of Kolb's four learning styles will be described more fully below.

Re 1 The dreamer

Dreamer

Dreamers are open to new experiences. A dreamer can effectively analyse and think about these experiences. Dreamers look at their experiences from different vantage points. They like to observe other people and situations. Once they go into action, they keep the insights of others in mind.

Strong points	*Weak points*
· Search for background information	· Hesitant
· Weigh the opinions of others	· Slow to take action
· Recognising and identifying problems	· Cannot see the wood for the trees
· Identifying differences between the desired and the current situation	· Not very critical

As a dreamer you learn the most when:
· You get the time to digest your observations
· You get a visual presentation of the study material
· You are able to listen and observe
· You write reports and analyses
· You do not experience pressure from outside

Re 2 The thinker

Thinker

Thinkers think problems through in a structured manner. A thinker is very capable of developing theories on the basis of a problem analysis. Logical reasoning and rational thinking are key words that are applicable to the thinker.

Strong points
- Formulating alternative solutions to problems
- Making use of experiences
- Logic and exactitude
- Organising and planning

Weak points
- Theory takes precedence over facts
- Avoidance of risks
- Not much sense of their own feelings and the feelings of others
- Minimal sense of reality

As a thinker you learn the most:
- With a clear-cut structure
- If you can investigate the basic points of the logic of something
- By mental exertion
- If you have space and time to think

Re 3 The decider

Decider

A decider is focused on the practical application of ideas. Deciders react quickly and are direct in their contact with others. The decider is a real problem-solver. He likes to work in situations in which only one answer to a question is possible.

Strong points
- Curious
- Decisive
- Testing solutions in practice
- Setting up goals and priorities

Weak points
- Impatient
- Very willing to spring into action
- Task takes precedence over people
- Not weighing alternatives

As a decider you learn most:
- If you can draw your own practical conclusions
- If the study materials are relevant to the practice
- By demonstration
- By trying out things, aided by an expert
- If you can be engaged in activities that yield a clear-cut result

Re 4 The doer

Doer

With a doer the emphasis is on concrete experiencing and active experimentation. Doers trust the information provided by others. They are orientated towards action and are constantly looking for new challenges.

Strong points
- Decisive
- Purposeful
- Intuitive
- Gets along with and motivates people very well

Weak points
- Impatient
- Fast quitter, does not finish his business
- Not interested in theories
- Bad organiser and planner

As a doer you learn most:
- In surroundings where you are constantly challenged
- When you are thrown in at the deep end
- If you can work closely together with others
- If there is enough variation in the curriculum or in your work

2.9   Active learning attitude and style

In the preceding section you were acquainted with Kolb's learning styles model and you performed your personal learning style test. In this section you will encounter a different learning style model. This model will yield different information about you than Kolb's model. Furthermore, the two learning styles dealt with here – the applicational and the experiential learning styles – will be viewed in combination with an active learning attitude. And an active learning attitude is very important in developing your competencies.

Competency-directed learning is more than merely acquiring passive knowledge that you will soon forget. After all, a competency is a professional competency: you can consider yourself competent when you are able to adequately perform certain specific professional activities. To do that you require a specific combination of knowledge, skills, attitude and behaviour (see Chapter 1).

How does this affect your learning style? In other words, with which demands must your learning style comply? To start with:
- You must be capable of learning to act on the basis of self-reflection. See Section 2.2.
- You must understand the nature of knowledge and be able to apply it in a practical way. Mere possession of knowledge is by no means proof of competency.

Transfer
- Of vital importance is transfer of knowledge. Being able to transfer knowledge means that you have understood and digested your learning experiences so thoroughly that you can also apply them to different situations. You can therefore also apply your learning experiences at school to a professional environment. Without the ability to transfer you cannot develop competencies.

We will consider three learning styles in this section. Which of these learning styles complies best with the demands postulated above?

Reproductive learning style

1 The first learning style is the reproductive learning style: learning by heart everything you hear in class and read in books. You need to reproduce all that knowledge in order to pass your exams. In the old way of teaching and learning, regurgitating knowledge was all-important. It can still be very useful when you do written exams. But for learning that is competency-directed (and therefore for competency management) this style of learning alone is insufficient because understanding and practical application form no part of it. Furthermore, no transfer of knowledge is required: the exercises taught are crammed in and forgotten very quickly.

Applicational learning style

2 The second applicational learning style forms part of a learning attitude that is job directed. Someone with this style of learning is mainly concerned with practical application. He or she will continually ask: 'How can I use this material?' or 'Of what practical use is it to me?' In posing these questions you immediately make everything relevant to practical professional performance. This is an ideal learning style for all courses which are directed towards specific jobs. As such, it is also pertinent to competency

management, because being able to utilise knowledge is essential to each competence. As such, this style of learning has much to recommend it. But it is not always an option because not all of the learning material you have to digest is immediately applicable. Sometimes certain materials cannot be applied practically and concretely because of the simple fact that you are not yet performing in a work situation. Sometimes you acquire general knowledge that is important to functioning better but that is not immediately practically applicable. Moreover, competencies entail more than just practical use. This is why you should combine the applicational learning style with the experiential style of learning.

Experiential

3 The final experiential learning style revolves around understanding and critical digestion of the material: making it your own in your own way. A person who adopts this style of learning is asking specifically for the 'why'. He or she is investigating connections, structures and contexts, not learning by rote but summarising it in his or her own words and analysing it. At the very least this person is always wondering 'what exactly does it say here?' The

Wh-questions

Wh-questions – what, when and why, as well as how and how much – are important. Those with an experiential learning style pose these questions in many situations, and question themselves in particular. And they are not easily satisfied with superficial answers: they realise that all these questions require thorough

Self-reflection

investigation. For self-reflection (see Section 2.2) this style of learning is very important. After all, it entails learning from your own experiences, which cannot be done without asking these questions. Because if you never think about what you actually do, how can you possibly ever learn from your experiences? This style

Transfer

of learning is also important for transfer: that is, the application and use of material in different situations. Material that you understand well and have properly summarised in your own words is ready to use whenever you feel it is necessary.

Competency management

Moreover, in competency management we are dealing with questions such as 'what do I want?', 'what can I do?' and so on. The third style of learning – the experiential style – is particularly appropriate for addressing such questions. There is also an obvious connection between this learning style and attitude and personal interest. People

Attitude and personal interest

who score high in the experiential learning style have a more inherent interest in their education than people with reproductive or applicational learning styles.

There are two aspects to this. Firstly, that inherent interest may be inherently part of the learning style in question. Those who are absolutely not interested in the material that forms part of their studies or in their job are unlikely to ask for the 'why'. But conversely, that learning style can also promote interest. Regularly asking for the whats and wherefores and constantly summarising things in your own words means that the material will truly become *your* material. If you understand the what and why of something it becomes interesting to you. Furthermore, the question 'what do I want?' is one that an experiential learning style is most capable of investigating. And the more you investigate that question the better you will know what is indeed motivating and what is not.

Active learning attitude

For competency management an active learning attitude is required. After all, you yourself have to develop your own competencies. To do so it is important to have a combination of the applicational and the experiential styles of learning: the applicational learning style because it helps you look for an answer to the question of practical implementation, and the experiential style of learning because it makes you investigate further the why, what and how.

Assignment 2.10 Exercises in the applicational learning style

Discuss with your teacher which assignments you will need to carry out for this and in which sequence. After consulting your study coach or tutor you may find yourself having to repeat certain assignments a few times in order to perfect this style of learning.

a Select a part of your studies which you find practical and useful and apply it to a situation outside of your studies. Write a brief report. In it, indicate which knowledge you applied and for which practical purpose. Also indicate in what way your proposals have worked in practice.
Suggestions for subjects:
- You could apply material from organisational theory by writing down a few suggestions for improving the organisation of your soccer team.
- You could apply lessons on creative training (or marketing, or commercial presentation) by creating an attractive brochure about your sports club or studies.
- You could apply lessons on website building by creating your own homepage.
- You could apply lessons on speaking skills by giving a public address.
- You could use an aspect of conflict management and negotiation by applying the methods learned in negotiating a holiday destination, the deployment of your sports team, or in another personal situation. Which tactics would you follow? Why?

b Take a look at all aspects of your studies and indicate which have the most practical use. Choose at least two. Indicate in detail what knowledge and which experiences you intend to use. Indicate precisely how you plan to apply them.
c Do a practical investigation of the assignment being carried out by your current project group. Discuss all knowledge aspects with your fellow students and reach agreement on how to apply them practically.
d Take a look at the next study term and choose the part you find most practical. Then indicate your targets: what knowledge do you want to acquire and what experiences would you like to have? What is the best way of applying this module to your experiences?

Assignment 2.11 Exercises in the experiential learning style

Discuss with your teacher which assignments you will need to carry out, and in which sequence. After consulting your study coach or tutor you may find that you will need to repeat certain assignments a few times in order to perfect this style of learning.

a Together with your fellow students investigate the 'why' and 'how' of the learning project you are performing. Think about the Wh-questions: what are the targets of the project? Which is the most important target? How do we reach those targets and what will this entail? How much time will it take? What do we want to attain personally (and so, what do we ourselves think most important?) How do we go about it? Do this at the beginning of the project. Write down all the answers, save them in the group's portfolio and check during the process whether the answers will have to be modified.

b Together with your fellow students investigate the 'why' of specific theories you have to study. Summarise in your own words what they are essentially about and what the essential points of the text are.

c While studying the course material, regularly ask yourself the 'why' question. Do this as follows:
- Stop reading when you reach the end of each page.
- Formulate the main conclusions from the text you have just finished reading: what is it saying exactly? Write this down.
- After you have read the entire text, reformulate the main conclusions of the text as a whole and write these down.
- Investigate any difficult pieces of text: what do you understand and what not? Write down a list of specific questions you plan to ask your teacher. These may be the Wh-questions, such as 'what does it actually say here?', 'How does that actually work?' and 'Can you give me an example?'

d Select a part of your studies (a module, a project) and indicate clearly what you want to learn, how you want to do that and why: what are your targets, why are they important to you, how do you plan to attain them, and what will you do and when?

Assignment 2.12 Personal learning styles test

By doing the learning styles test you will discover what your preferred style of learning is. You will find the test in Appendix 2 'Learning styles test'.

Fill in the test according to the instructions and do the following assignments:
a What is your preferred style of learning?
b Describe two learning situations from practice showing that this style of learning is indeed your preferred way of learning.
c Describe two learning situations from practice in which you found it hard to learn something new.
d Describe what you plan to do to make your way of learning more effective.

 Make a report of this assignment in your PDP Toolbox in the Assignments section.

2.10 Your personal development plan

Once you have completed all the previous exercises you may feel dizzy from all the core qualities, personality traits, learning styles, standards and values you may have. Or from the types you may be, the reformer, helper, challenger, but also the dreamer or thinker. Remember that all these type descriptions and tests are tools and that they do not represent an absolute truth. Hopefully, a perfectionist also has a number of the characteristics of a helper, and vice versa. It would be a bad thing if you decided on the basis of the test results that 'I really cannot chair the meeting because according to my Enneagram test I am an observer'. Your aim should be to acquire for yourself and your future career, precisely those qualities you do not yet possess.

Through doing all the assignments you will have acquired a realistic impression of yourself. You will know who you are, what you can do, and what your strong and weak points are. You will know what is important to you. You will know where you stand and where you want to go. This is the right time to start with your personal development plan, your PDP.

Assignment 2.13 Updating your personality profile

Begin by reading through all the reports you made of the assignments in this chapter. Proceed to the part Personality Profile of the PDP Toolbox and fill in everything you can fill in on the basis of the completed assignments.

Assignment 2.14 Updating your PDP action points and logbook

Whilst doing the assignments in this book, you will often find that you will have to acquire knowledge and skills, and to make your professional attitude professional, i.e., you will have to work on your competencies. To achieve this, you can systematically set up action points for yourself. During and after completing these action points you can keep tabs on your progress in a logbook (a sort of report). Section 6.2 gives an example of this.

Read through the assignments you have done in this chapter. Set up a list of action points and enter these in your personal file or the PDP Toolbox under the heading PDP action points and logbook. The Toolbox also allows you to enter a final date for an action point, enabling you to keep up a plan of action and monitor your progress.

What can I do as an individual?

3

In this chapter you will investigate what you can do as an individual.
We will focus on skills in particular. In the next chapter we will focus
on what you can do in a group.

The first section of this chapter is about taking stock of what you
already can do at the beginning of your studies. You will investigate
your strong and weak points specifically, and how you can improve
those weak (or not so strong!) points. The following section focusses
on investigating your progress in the first year of study.
Sections 3.3 to 3.5 are about investigating which kind of person you
are, and what types of behaviour you exhibit. In Section 3.5 your
basic behaviour (or your 'natural' behaviour) is compared with your

behaviour in work situations and at school, your so-called response behaviour.

Sections 3.6 and 3.7 are about being proactive and about formulating your own targets. Better time management (dealt with in 3.8) will be a consequence, as will an ability to establish priorities (3.9). Section 3.10 is about drawing up schedules, and how to adjust them is dealt with in 3.10.

In these sections, learning work experiences – such as internships and projects – are investigated. You will interview an intern, prepare your own internship and assess your own work learning experience.

Section 3.14 deals with how you can investigate your own motivation in connexion with dear personal targets and your knowledge, skills and attitude.

A higher education level of thinking and working may be expected from a higher education student. Section 3.15 investigates how far you meet this level.

Section 3.16 deals with making a personality profile. Section 3.17 investigates which professional competencies you possess sufficiently, and which will have to be developed further.

The final section deals with reviewing the results of the assignments in this chapter.

3.1 What can I do already?

You will do the first assignment in this chapter at the beginning of your studies: you will list what you expect from your education and what your strong and weak points are. In fact, this is the first stocktaking of your competencies, and of your skills in particular.

Zero measurement   Taking stock of a starting point is known as a zero measurement. In the following assignments you will constantly assess your performance over a longer period of time. They include various assignments dealing with your functioning within groups and with these assignments in particular you will use the feedback of fellow students and teachers.

Assignment 3.1 is meant for first year students. It must be completed at the beginning of your studies, or even before: for example, during the initial interview with the teacher or tutor. Managing your competencies starts on day one of your studies, possibly even before that. For this reason, right at the beginning of your studies you will be given an assignment focusing on what you expect to gain from your studies, your strong and weak points, and the relevancy to your future profession. This is an immediate assessment of competencies. The aim is to get an answer to the question 'What can I do already?' right at the start of your studies. By comparing these results with results from later assignments, you and your teachers will be able to measure your rate of progress with accuracy.

Assignment 3.1 Zero measurement

Complete the following assignments:

a List your strong points and your weaker points. Provide an explanation and examples! Approach the task as follows:
  - Describe four situations (at school or in your private life) in which you performed well. Be brief but specific. State clearly why you were satisfied with your performance.
  - Describe two situations (at school or in your private life) in which you performed poorly. Be brief but specific.

b Why did you choose this course and this school? Indicate (if possible) what kind of profession or what kind of work appeals to you.

c Indicate briefly what you expect from this school with respect to:
  - subjects on offer
  - amount of study time
  - support given by teachers or mentors.

d List at least two courses in this training that suit you and at least two courses that you find less suitable.

e State your main study targets. Make sure to list action points you intend to focus on and why.

Save your answers carefully; it will be useful to compare them with the answers to the following assignments.

 Enter the answers to *a* in your PDP Toolbox in the Personality profile section. Enter the answers to *b, c* and *d* in the Assignments section. Enter the action points you formulated for *e* under the PDP Action points section and in the logbook of the PDP Toolbox.

3.2 How far have I progressed?

At the beginning of your studies and after reading the first section (3.1) and doing Assignment 3.1, you will have made a so-called zero measurement. In learning about managing your competencies it is useful to record your progress occasionally, which is why Assignment 3.2 is about assessing how far you progressed with your competencies in the first year of your studies. It is very useful to compare the answers from this assignment with those of Assignment 3.1, the 'zero measurement'.

It is also useful to repeat the assignment a few times during the course of your studies, or indeed, even in your later profession. Jobs change constantly, and each change will yield a different perspective on your strengths and weaknesses.

Assignment 3.2 Self-reflection halfway through the first year of studies

Complete the following assignments:

a Set up an actualised personality profile in the PDP Toolbox. If you do not use the Toolbox, write a curriculum vitae according to the division in Section 6.9.

b Make a strength-weakness analysis and in it identify which strong points (at least four) you have shown so far during your studies, and which points for improvement (at least two) have suggested themselves. Give clear examples! Approach the task as follows:
   - List your strongest points
   - Provide examples and proofs of these strong points

Describe situations during your studies in which you performed well. They may include exams, individual assignments, group assignments, and so on, as long as they are clearly related to your studies. Provide a brief but specific description of the situations and state clearly why you are satisfied with these performances. You can also provide any assessments by teachers and fellow students. Gather as many specific *pieces of evidence* as possible and keep these in your portfolio. Pieces of evidence may consist of test results, written evaluations, professional products such as reports and presentations, and so on.
   - List your weakest points
   - Provide examples of these weak points

Describe situations during your studies in which you performed poorly. Give a brief but specific description and also provide any assessments by teachers and fellow students.
   - Finally, provide an overall judgement. When comparing your strong and weak points, were you satisfied or not? In your view so far, have you performed well? Please provide a brief explanation.

c Set up your first professional competency profile. Approach the task as follows:
   - Determine the competencies specific to your studies (in the study guide or the training profile. Consult your teacher, if necessary).
   - List two competencies (at least) that suit you best and provide examples/arguments why.
   - List two competencies (at least) that suit you least and again provide examples/arguments why. Try to back them up with some evidence.

d The strength-weakness analysis and professional competency profile will have yielded points for improvement. This raises a question: 'What do I still have to do?' Formulate your study targets on the basis of this, indicating which weak points you intend to improve, and in which way. Follow the method described in Section 6.1, Study targets in four steps.

 Enter this part of the assignment in your PDP Toolbox in the PDP Action points section and in the logbook.

e Compare your answers from this assignment with those of Assignment 3.1, the 'zero measurement'.

Enter the answers to *a* and *b* in your PDP Toolbox in the Personality profile section. Enter the professional competency profile of *c* in the Competencies and competency profile section. Indicate that these entries relate to a professional competency.

Enter the improvement points formulated for *d* as action points under the PDP Action points section and in the logbook of the PDP Toolbox. Enter the comparison of point *e* in the Assignments section.

3.3 Four behavioural types

Everyone behaves differently. One person acts on the basis of his feelings, another more rationally. One may be an extrovert, another an introvert. Obviously, this will influence someone's competencies. An extrovert person will have different strengths and weaknesses to those of an introvert. His attitude will be different as well, and he will have different personality traits. Consequently, it is useful for your competency management to investigate which type of behaviour you exhibit.

MDI

These matters are dealt with using the MDI (Management Development Instrument), or the MDI behaviour analysis. This analysis demonstrates how we approach the world around us and how we react to our environment, whether it be work or home. This tool identifies four psychological types and four types of behaviour. Assignment 3.3 is about investigating which types fit you best. Assignment 3.4 is about investigating the behaviour colour that fits you. In the following chapter, Section 4.6 is about investigating the consequences of this behaviour for teamwork.

The MDI behaviour analysis distinguishes 'introverts' and 'extroverts', and also 'thinkers' and 'feelers' (Bonstetter et al, 1993).

Introverts

Introverts function best in isolation. They feel most at ease when they are alone and are left in peace. They like to take plenty of time to think things over, and prefer to do so in solitude. They prefer 'one to one contact' to contacts with larger groups. They are particularly systematic, fact-focused, and conservative: they like to hold on to what is already there.

Extroverts

Extroverts function best when they have contact with others. They feel most at ease when they have a lot of people around them. When they are tired, they go out with friends or ring people up; this is their way of recharging themselves. They think while they are talking (whereas introverts always think first), and they love brainstorming. Unlike introverts, they love change; they are more creative and open to new or different ideas.

Thinkers

Thinkers decide by logic. They have feelings, but mainly make decisions based on analysis and logic. They can be convinced only by well-founded and logical arguments. They want to see facts and numbers, and not subjective ideas. They focus more on a given task than on relationships and will, therefore, never change their minds to please someone else. They strive for objectivity.

Feelers

Feelers decide with their heart. They can, of course, think as well as anyone, but their decisions are based on their feelings. They can suddenly change their opinions on the basis of feelings (whereas a thinker needs arguments). They focus more on relationships than on given tasks and will, therefore, change their minds to please someone else. Their decisions are fairly subjective and personal.

Introverts often think extroverts are superficial, because extroverts will often just blurt something out. 'Why don't you stop and think first?' an introvert will say. Extroverts often feel that introverts are slow because they take so long to think and are so careful. 'Why do you take so long to think? Why don't you say what you think?' the extrovert will say. Thinkers find feelers undependable: why do they change their opinion without objective arguments? Feelers find thinkers cool and arrogant: why are they always so businesslike, and why do you have to bring up so many arguments to convince them? Yet, the one is not better than the other. Feelers have different strengths to thinkers and extroverts have different strengths to introverts.

In the following assignment you will investigate what you are: introvert or extrovert, thinker or feeler. You will also investigate which strengths and weaknesses are involved.

Assignment 3.3 Introvert or extrovert, thinking or feeling?
a In work situations (at school, during projects, etc) indicate which applies most to you: introvert or extrovert. A combination of both is possible. Provide arguments and examples.
b In work situations (at school, during projects, et cetera) indicate which applies most to you: thinking or feeling. A combination of both is possible. Provide arguments and examples.
c Provide examples of some of your strong and some weaker points relating to this situation. If you are an 'introvert' and a 'thinker' indicate the strong and weak points that are a direct result of that.
d Ask for feedback on all these issues from at least two fellow students who know you well and who have worked with you (see Section 6.4, Receiving feedback). Discuss the following:
   · Do they think you are an introvert or extrovert? (A combination is possible.) Ask them to explain.
   · Do they think you are a thinker or a feeler? (A combination is possible.) Ask them to explain.
   · Ask them to give you examples of at least two strengths and two weaknesses related to this.
   Indicate to what extent you agree with this feedback.

 Make a report of this assignment in your PDP Toolbox in the Assignments section.

3.4   Four behavioural colours

The MDI (Management Development Instrument) is based on the distinction between introvert, extrovert, thinking and feeling (see the previous section). There is a further division into four types of behaviour: Dominance (fiery red), Influence (sunny yellow), Stability (earthy green) and Conformity (cool blue). Each type is related to specific strengths and weaknesses, a specific attitude and specific personality traits, and they can be found in every situation, including work situations.

Dominance (red)

Red

The behaviour type Dominance – represented by the colour red – is found among Extroverts and Thinkers. This type is also known as the 'intuitive thinker'. Basic characteristics: dynamism, anger. A person with a dominant style of behaviour is a clear-cut leader: a powerful, demanding, dominant and fairly headstrong personality. He reacts actively to problems and challenges. Winning is everything to him: he is extremely focused on results. He wants to see specific results, and attain specific (and ambitious) goals. He is geared to efficiency: everything has to happen faster and better. This is why he often takes the initiative to start activities. He thinks quickly and makes decisions quickly. Often he will be the first one to say 'this is how we are going to go about it'.

He is also courageous and strong-willed. He has a short fuse, but forgets his anger quickly. He is often brutally honest, straightforward, and sometimes too dominant. He is adventurous, direct, innovative, more focused on results than on people (and consequently more businesslike than personal), determined and a problem-solver. His solutions are logical and astute, and often imaginative and unusual. He is looking for the unusual, the adventurous. He is not interested in arguments such as 'but we have always done it this way': everything always has to be done differently. He is an independent thinker, not someone who wants to do what others are doing. He loves challenges and 'important' assignments that allow him to grow. He takes a lot of risks because his goals are very ambitious. It is not for nothing that this style has fiery red as its colour.

Attention points: he does not listen very well, frightens others with his directness, should show appreciation more often, should make concessions to others more often, uses his power too much, is not tactful, comes across as aggressive without being aware of it, often hurries others (and himself) too often, sometimes reaches too far and takes on too much, is himself motivated by fierce discussion, but frightens others with his, often goes against the team's interests, quickly spots the 'main points' but easily loses sight of details.

Ideal work environment: little control or supervision, innovative and future oriented, a forum to express ideas and opinions, varied work, no detailed work, challenges and opportunities.

Famous 'red' people: John McEnroe (tennis player), Alex Ferguson (soccer manager). 'Red' types are often good crisis managers.

Influence (yellow)

Yellow

The behaviour type Influence – represented by the colour yellow – is found among Extroverts and Feelers. Basic characteristics: boundless optimism and enthusiasm. Someone who scores high on this style is an inspirer: extroverted, kind, friendly and convincing. He is optimistic, enthusiastic and creative. He is a real talker who believes in his product – he can sell a complete bike to someone who just wants a bicycle tire, simply by his enthusiasm. He always works on a lot of things simultaneously, precisely because he can be enthusiastic about so many of them. He motivates others to attain their goals, and is an obvious team player. He also knows how to solve (and mediate in) conflicts. He is charming, self-assured, popular and sociable. He is often very funny, which is good for the general atmosphere. He is always positive. He is a good talker, and consequently promotes his ideas very well. He is quick to make contacts and stimulates other people. He will rarely oppose others wilfully because he wants to be liked by everyone. He is adventurous and not afraid of risks, extremely spontaneous and always wanting to improve the world. This behaviour has sunny yellow as its colour.

Attention points: often does not concentrate enough on what he is engaged in because he is thinking of a hundred different things, is too noisy, often in his optimism overestimates his own and other's capabilities, overlooks many details, is often not very realistic because of his optimism, drives others crazy with his optimism and enthusiasm, trusts others immediately and too quickly, listens one minute and not the next, must manage his time better and set up priorities.

Ideal work environment: contact with lots of people, little control and freedom of movement, a forum to listen to ideas and opinions, prefers a democratic manager he has a good relationship to.

Famous 'yellow' people: Clinton (ex-president USA), Eddy Murphy (comedian). 'Yellow' types are often good comics and salespeople.

Stability (green)

Green

The behaviour type Stability – colour green – is found among Introverts and Feelers. Basic characteristics: striving for harmony, unwillingness to show emotions. A person who scores high in this style is a supporter: a kind, friendly, quiet and gentle person who gets along well with others. He is very sympathetic and encouraging. He is someone who often asks: 'How are you?' and 'shall we do that together?' He is moderate, self-controlled, attentive, patient, trustworthy and methodical. He is also very loyal: he is always willing to help friends and colleagues. He is always of service to colleagues and the boss, and committed to achieving the final goal. He wants to keep his work environment like himself: predictable, without too many changes or any upheaval. He is always looking for approval and is slow to adjust to changes. He is very good in specialised work that demands a consistent performance level. He works slowly and systematically, logically and step by step; he will finish a task completely before taking on the next one. He will never do too many things simultaneously. In this way he maintains a clear picture of events, the routine and the pattern. He is very accepting and easy to get along with. He is very good with people, not in the least because he is very relaxed and patient. He is never hurried. He looks at things from all sides. He is a good listener, sympathetic, calm and stabilising.

Attention points: sometimes gives in too quickly (wants to maintain harmony and therefore evades conflict), has difficulty in setting up priorities because he is unsure of what he really wants, has problems with unannounced changes and unpredictable situations, loses sight of the overview when confronted with various situations, sometimes works slowly and takes little or no initiative, has little feeling for urgency, is oversensitive to criticism (takes it as a personal attack), is very worried about what others think, is sometimes stubborn and hostile to sudden changes (says 'yes', but acts 'no') because he wants to find out first what the changes will mean to him and his environment.

Ideal work environment: stable and predictable, sufficient attention for himself and much appreciation for tasks completed carefully, an environment allowing him to complete his tasks fully (no rough and ready work in view of deadlines), precise criteria, patterns and procedures, plenty of time to adapt to changes.

Famous 'green' people: Matlock (lawyer in a TV series), Gandhi (pacifist activist in India). 'Green' types often are good teachers and helpful instructors.

Conformity (blue)

Blue

Blue is the colour of behaviour type Conformity, which is found among Introverts and Thinkers. Basic characteristic: perfectionism. Someone scoring high in this behaviour is an observer: precise, careful, disciplined and extremely conscientious. He will always want to complete his tasks down to the smallest detail: not being exact troubles his conscience. Only perfection is good enough. He has very critical observational powers and will always demand well-founded arguments. He will ask questions such as: 'What exactly are the agreements?', 'When does it have to be finished?', or 'May I please have an exact plan of attack?' He is very objective, goes 'by the book', always reflects carefully and prepares very thoroughly for everything because he is afraid of making a fool of himself. He will test and check everything and will always ask pertinent critical questions. He pays a lot of attention to details. He avoids emotions and will certainly not show them. He looks for 'the right answer', reflects on it at length and will gather plenty of factual material, and he will often avoid having to make decisions. He is afraid of making mistakes, and even more afraid of admitting them. He looks for people like him, and for a quiet and stable environment. He is cool and not very sympathetic, often does not react, or only slowly. That is because he approaches things as an objective observer. He will always remain calm, does not care for status or money, and is good at looking at things 'from a distance', hence the colour blue, which represents equanimity and coolness.

Attention points: sometimes does not take enough risks because he does everything 'according to the book', sometimes does not respond adequately, comes across as emotionless, does not question enough what he wants and what his limitations are, can be defensive and cynical, is easily pressured when he does not know or like people, sometimes gets upset when less intelligent people score better because of their greater social skills, has trouble explaining what he wants, does not stand up for himself sufficiently.

Ideal work environment: close ties with a small group of like-minded people, tasks demanding critical thinking, technical or specialised work, familiar work surroundings with his own office or work space, clearly formulated procedures, good availability of data and information, time to reflect and complete everything carefully, an environment where quality and objective problem solving are appreciated.

Famous 'blue' people: Mr Spock (the emotionless character in Star Trek). 'Blue' types often are good controllers, bookkeepers and administrators.

In reality, everybody exhibits a combination of these four behaviour types. This combination is analysed very carefully in the MDI-scan, and evaluated with a certified trainer. You will find more information about this on www.mdi.nl. You must take the MDI scan for an exact measurement; consult your teachers about this. Do the following assignment for a global picture.

Assignment 3.4 Which colour are you?

a Which type (or types) of behaviour do you recognise most in yourself? Concentrate in particular on your behaviour at school and in work situations. Explain and give examples. Discuss the similarities between you and the behaviour described, and also the differences.

b Which of the strengths and weaknesses belonging to that type (or types) do you recognise in yourself? Concentrate in particular on school and work situations. Explain and give examples.

c Comment on 'the ideal work environment' described for your most characteristic type(s). Is what it says correct for you or not? Explain your reasons. Indicate which type of work really suits your character.

d Ask for feedback on all this from at least two students who know you well and who have worked with you (see Section 6.4, Receiving feedback). Discuss the following:
  · Which type or types of behaviour do they think is representative of you? Ask them to explain.
  · Ask them to identify at least two strengths and two weaknesses related to that type or types of behaviour.

e Then indicate to what extent you agree with this feedback.

 Make a report of this assignment in your PDP Toolbox in the Assignments section.

3.5   Basic behaviour versus response behaviour

You may behave quite differently at school and at work from the way you behave at home. Many people are completely different at work than in the pub or at home on the sofa. In view of this, it is important to make the distinction between basic behaviour and response behaviour.

Response behaviour

Response behaviour is sometimes called masked behaviour (Bonnstetter et al, 1993). 'Response' means 'answer': response behaviour is behaviour that answers questions put to someone at work or at school. It is the behaviour we exhibit in reaction to the environment. A chairman is expected to behave calmly and formally, and that is why he behaves in that manner, although in reality he may not be like that at all. A student who is normally quite rambunctious during his internship, will suddenly address everybody in a calm and polite manner. This sort of adjusted behaviour is called response behaviour.

Basic behaviour

Basic behaviour is our most natural style of behaviour: the behaviour we exhibit when we do not adapt it to the situation. Therefore, it is the behaviour we show when we are truly ourselves, and when the environment does not require us to adapt: for example, the way we are at home, relaxing with a partner, or in the pub, with friends, or during breaks between lectures at school, with friends in the canteen. Basic behaviour corresponds to our 'true self'. We exhibit this when we are completely relaxed, though basic behaviour will also emerge under heavy pressure. When someone is 'fed up', he may simply not have the energy to continue to adapt to the situation, and then his basic behaviour emerges.

Response behaviour is not fixed. After all, in each new situation people readapt. Basic behaviour actually hardly changes at all, only when someone goes through a major crisis such as a divorce, or when a loved one passes away.

In Section 3.4 we mentioned the MDI scan: this scan measures the difference between response behaviour and basic behaviour. This test is very useful for obtaining an accurate picture. The following assignment is meant for a more global picture. But a global picture is useful as well. To take an example: by nature someone is very 'yellow', i.e. very enthusiastic, noisy and optimistic, but at his work really fairly quiet and quite careful. This could mean that his 'normal' strengths and weaknesses do not show at his workplace at all. It could mean that he is trying too hard to fit in, or trying in the wrong way. How about you? What are your strengths and weaknesses when you are 'yourself'? What are your strengths and weaknesses when you are at school?

Assignment 3.5 Comparing your response behaviour with your basic behaviour

a   Read the theory in Section 3.4, Four behaviour colours.

b   Discuss your response behaviour. Indicate which type of behaviour (red, yellow, green or blue) you recognise most in yourself. Concentrate on your behaviour at school and in work situations. Explain and give examples.

c   Which strengths and weaknesses do you exhibit most at school? Concentrate in particular on strengths and weaknesses related to the type of behaviour that fits you best.

d   Discuss your basic behaviour. Now indicate which type of behaviour (red, yellow, green or blue) you recognise most, but concentrate in particular on your 'natural' behaviour at home, in the pub, together with friends, etc).

e   Enumerate the main differences and similarities between your basic behaviour and response behaviour, and also differences not directly related to the MDI theory.

f   Ask for feedback on all these matters (see Section 6.4, Receiving feedback). Ask for feedback on your response behaviour from a student (which type of behaviour does he recognise in you whilst at school, which strengths and weaknesses), and ask one member of your family for feedback on your response behaviour (which type of behaviour does he recognise in you during leisure situations, and which strengths and weaknesses).

g   Finally, record your conclusions. Look at your response behaviour (including strengths and weaknesses), your basic behaviour (including strengths and weaknesses) and the differences between them. What is most striking? Which are the most notable strengths? Which things do you need to change? How are you going to do that?

 Make a report of this assignment in your PDP Toolbox in the Assignments section.

3.6   Being proactive

Being proactive and identifying targets are very important to competency management. Not being proactive means that you lack initiative and are insufficiently interested in your own development. Without targets you may be actively engaged, but you will not have a clear sense of direction. In this section we not only elucidate the concept of being proactive, but also the opposite: being reactive. In the following section we will deal further with the setting up of targets.

Being proactive   Being proactive is not only a question of skill but also (and more specifically) of attitude: an awareness of controlling your own life and of being personally responsible for your own failure or success – you and no one else. You do not attend a project group meeting with the idea of 'I'll see what happens' but because you really want to accomplish something. If something goes wrong you do not point the finger at a hundred others but you begin to investigate seriously what you can do differently.

Proactive

Reactive

Covey (2005) points out the importance of the difference between proactive behaviour and reactive behaviour. Proactive behaviour means making your own choices and looking ahead. You do not wait for things to happen to you but instead take the initiative yourself. You think before you act. This gives you more control, even when something unexpected happens! Reactive behaviour means you merely react to things and follow your impulses. You lack control because you let yourself be controlled. The circumstances determine what you feel: others determine what you will do.

Reactive individuals

Reactive individuals often think and say the following:

· That's how I am and there's nothing I can do about it.
· Well, I'll give it a try...but I don't know if it will work...
· I have no choice, do I?
· I can't do it. I give up.
· My day is ruined and you're to blame.

Reactive individuals display the following characteristics:
· They are easily insulted.
· In the face of adversity they lose their composure very quickly.
· They are quick to blame others and do not investigate what they can do themselves.
· When they are criticised they say: 'Yes, but...' without actually taking the criticism on board.
· All too often they wait passively for something to happen.
· They only change their behaviour when they have absolutely no other choice.

Proactive individuals

Proactive individuals think and say things such as:
· It is my own choice.
· I must be able to do this better.
· There must be a way...I won't give up.
· I will not just try to do it, *I will* do it.

Proactive persons display the following characteristics:
· They are not easily insulted.
· They are unperturbed in the face of adversity.
· They take responsibility for their own choices and do not point the finger at others.
· They seriously examine any criticism by others.
· They act on their own initiative and actively look for ways to get something done.
· They take the initiative to change their own behaviour if they think that is necessary.
· They only focus on things they can influence and do not allow themselves to be fooled by things they cannot influence.

Of course, no one is a hundred percent proactive. Still, it is a good thing to be as proactive as possible. Because otherwise your choices are not fully your own choices!

Assignment 3.6 How proactive am I really?

a Check the characteristics of proactive behaviour described above and use examples to show which ones you most recognise in yourself. When did you really take charge yourself? How?

b Check the characteristics of reactive behaviour described above and use examples to show which ones you most recognise in yourself. When did you not take the initiative and left it to others to do so?

c Compare *a* and *b* and indicate whether you find yourself sufficiently proactive. Do you think you take charge sufficiently and show enough initiative? What has gone well in that respect and what can be improved? Explain.

d Gather feedback: have some fellow students comment briefly on whether they find you proactive or not. Ask them to clarify their statements. Indicate also if, based on this feedback, you can identify extra areas for improvement or not.

e End by drawing up a brief plan of action: indicate which strengths you would like to develop further and which areas of improvement you intend to tackle. Indicate also how you plan to do that.

Assignment 3.7 Keeping a logbook on being proactive

a Check the instructions in Section 6.2 (Points of action and logbook) and set up a 'logbook self-evaluation'. Insert two headings in the book: proactive and reactive.

b Write entries in this logbook for a month. Each week enter examples of proactive behaviour and of reactive behaviour. Also provide brief evaluations of these instances of behaviour.

c A month later, write a report based on this logbook. Indicate briefly which are your strong points and which your weak points. Refer as clearly as possible to specific examples in your logbook. Also evaluate whether you are satisfied or not, which study targets are still unmet, and how you plan to complete them.

Assignment 3.8 Take the initiative: develop your competencies!

a Identify a competency you would really like to develop further this year. Also indicate why you wish to do so.

b State what initiatives you will take to develop it. Make use of 6.1 (Study targets in four steps). With those study targets in mind, put special emphasis on *initiatives* and show that is *you* who is taking charge.

c In developing your competencies, reconsider your knowledge, skills, attitude and behaviour. Indicate what results you want to achieve and how you intend to demonstrate that you have achieved them (e.g. specific test results, particular products, etc).

d After a discussion with your teacher, carry out your plan. In the meantime, evaluate whether your progress is satisfactory. Take the initiative *yourself* to change things if necessary. Consult your teacher about these matters as well.

e Finally, evaluate whether you have succeeded. Do this together with your teacher. Did you expand your competency sufficiently? Did you take enough initiative? And what might you still have to do?

3.7   Formulating targets

If you are proactive (see preceding section) you are taking full responsibility for your own actions. But you must do so purposefully, by setting up targets! Competency management is impossible without being proactive and having clearly defined targets. Moreover, without specific targets, you cannot know what direction to take, which then gives others the opportunity to determine that for you. People who have finished a course of higher education are expected to be able to determine their own direction. The ability to set targets is an important denominator of successful higher education, both during and after the studies.

Setting targets means knowing in which direction you want to go. You should only start when you can clearly visualise what your actions will lead to. Covey (2005) calls this 'Beginning with the end in mind'. Before you start to build a house you should first make a floor plan; before you start to bake a cake you should read a recipe, and before you start anything of any kind, you should make a plan. In this book we explain how to make your study targets specific, segmented, measurable and attainable: see Section 6.1. In this section we will investigate two special kinds of targets: the personal manifesto and specific targets.

Personal manifesto   The personal manifesto is a fundamental rule, a broadly formulated target which co-ordinates all your specific targets. Indicate in a few words or sentences what you want to reach and what your main values are. You could compare what you are doing to drawing up a constitution or to formulating a company's mission.

A personal manifesto can take many forms. It is of great importance that the manifesto clarifies what is important to *you*. Let us give you a few tips:
· In Assignment 2.8 you should set up a top-ten of personal values. This could serve very well as a personal manifesto. You then plan for *everything* you need to do to live up to that top-ten of values.
· You could also enumerate your core qualities (see Section 2.4) in catch words: for example, 'decisive, result-oriented and hard working.' Those words could do good service as a personal manifesto. What you are in effect saying is 'Whatever I do, I will *always* adopt an attitude of being decisive, result-oriented and hard-working'.
· It could also be a simple motto: 'Honesty is the best policy', or 'I will face all obstacles with optimism', or 'Enthusiasm above all', or 'People are more important than results', or, conversely, 'Results are more important than people'.

- It could also be a personal rule of life, or even a number of rules, such as 'Trust yourself and your fellow man', 'Respect all opinions but also stand up for yourself', 'Always aim for the best result' and so on.

General target

As you see, a personal manifesto can take many different forms. And, of course, your personal manifesto will change over the years. But whatever the form, it is always a general target that you should be focussing on in all concrete and specific situations.

Specific targets

However, having a personal manifesto is not enough. You need to also formulate specific targets for specific situations. Specific targets are a practical and specific elaboration of your personal manifesto. Let us say that your manifesto is to be 'decisive, results-oriented and hard-working'. You will then have to plan some specific actions with specific targets that match this manifesto. So set yourself a few decisive, results-oriented and hard-working goals with very specific final targets. These could include a well-written paper or a high exam score.

Four-step method

In Section 6.1 you will find a four-step method for formulating study targets correctly. You should also apply this method to specific targets: make them specific, divisible, measurable and attainable. Or in SMART target terms: Specific, Measurable, Attainable, Realistic, Time-related.

Two remarks:
- Without a proactive stance it is impossible to formulate targets. Conversely, without targets your proactive stance will not be proactive enough. Being proactive and setting targets are therefore mutually reinforcing.
- A personal manifesto without specific targets is too general an aim. But if you only have specific targets, you will drown in details: you need a general target which connects all the specific targets. This is why the personal manifesto and specific targets reinforce one another.

In competency management we are dealing with questions such as 'Who am I?', 'What should I do now?', 'Where do I fit in?' and 'What do I want?' All these questions become a lot more resolvable if you are proactive, have formulated a personal mission, and have set specific targets.

Assignment 3.9 Formulating a personal manifesto
a Firstly, enumerate three competencies that are important to your studies and your career. Briefly describe them.
b Also enumerate your main qualities. Check Section 2.4 ('Core qualities') for this. You could also sum up your strongest points and your main study targets.
c Enumerate your main values. See also Section 2.6 on values and motives.
d Next, formulate your manifesto. Indicate why this is your manifesto and also give some examples of recent initiatives that provide evidence of this manifesto.

e Make something creative – a web page, a poster, a brochure – to visualise this manifesto and to present it to others. In doing so, consider special fonts and illustrations (photographs, logos and the like) that indicate what you stand for.

Assignment 3.10 The group's manifesto and vision: comparing manifestos

a Compare your manifesto – see the assignment above – with the manifestos of your fellow group members (e.g. team mates in a project team). Also note which values and standards and which qualities are prevalent.
b Formulate a group manifesto; a kind of vision of the group as a whole. What does the group stand for? What is the common higher goal, what are the main values and standards? Provide a few examples of initiatives to take in order to reach this goal.
c Make something creative – a web page, a poster, a brochure – to visualise this manifesto and to present it to others. In doing so, consider special fonts and illustrations (photographs, logos and the like) that indicate what the group stands for.

Assignment 3.11 Formulating your targets

a Briefly formulate your manifesto.
b Then indicate what you specifically want to achieve between now and a point in time at least four weeks from now. Also indicate why you want to achieve this (your motivation, the importance of this target for your studies, its relationship to your manifesto, etc.).
c Next, formulate your targets according to the four-step method (see Section 6.1). That is, make them specific, divisible and attainable.

Assignment 3.12 Group targets

a Formulate the manifesto and vision of the group. Provide arguments for them.
b Next, formulate the specific targets of the group according to the four-step method (see Section 6.1) Also indicate why these targets are so important and why you as a group have chosen these targets.
c In formulating these targets also specify the individual responsibilities: who does what? Who has which specific tasks?

3.8 Time management

To attain your study and personal targets it is important to manage your time effectively and efficiently. Effectiveness and efficiency, moreover, are crucial aspects of every competency: someone who works ineffectively and inefficiently is by definition not very

Effective

Efficient

competent. To be effective means you spend your time on targets that are important at that moment: what you do has the desired effect and hits the desired target. To be efficient is to do something with the smallest amount of resources and exertion. When you do something efficiently, you usually need less time for it. If you want to cook a dish of macaroni efficiently, you will put on a pan of water for the pasta just before your pasta sauce has finished cooking. Efficiency often relates to the sequence in which you do things. It may appear logical to write an internship report at the end of the internship, but it is much more efficient to start writing the report during the internship. Minutes of a meeting are written most efficiently immediately after the meeting. However, you can do wrong things very efficiently too. For example, painting a shed with the least amount of effort could be termed working efficiently, but did you work effectively?

Section 6.7 provides tips on time management.

Assignment 3.13 Where does my time go?
To use your time well, you need to know what consumes your time.
a Study Section 6.7, Time management, carefully.
b What does 'using your time well' mean? Indicate what it means to you, and state clearly what your top priorities are.
c Estimate the amount of time you spend on all sorts of activities during the course of a week. For example, think of things such as sleeping, eating, being at school, home studies, work, friends.
d Describe five situations in which you waste time.
e Describe five situations in which you can improve your productivity.
f Think about what you have to do in the coming week. Make a schedule for these activities in your diary. Do not forget to calculate time for any preparation work. Make a mental note to make a new schedule on Monday of the following week.
g Which five tips from the list of tips in Section 6.7, Time management, are most useful to you?

h Use the time registration function of the PDP Toolbox for a week to record what you spend your time on each day. Of course, you may do this for more than one week. The Toolbox enables you to display your use of time graphically (click the button Show Graph).
i Compare the estimate of point c with the factual measurement of point h. At which points does your estimate deviate? What is causing this?

Some activities are more important than others. Some situations call for direct action because they are urgent. Others are less urgent and can wait a while. However, urgent does not necessarily mean important. For example, if during dinner you are phoned by a telepollster, that may seem urgent at that moment as, after all, the phone is ringing. But the phone call itself is likely to be completely unimportant to you. In Figure 3.1 you can put answering this call upper left.

j Think of a number of activities for your studies, your work or your private life, and enter these into the Time Quadrant chart of Figure 3.1.

Figure 3.1 Time quadrant chart

	Not urgent	Urgent
Unimportant		
Important		

k Give a brief characterisation of each quadrant in the diagram. Next to it write down how you would like to manage the activities in each quadrant.

l Based on your findings at *j* and *k*, indicate if you are working on the right things.

 Make a report of this assignment in your PDP Toolbox in the Assignments section.

3.9   Establishing priorities: procrastinators, yes-men, wasters and planners

In Section 3.8 we discussed the time quadrant chart. This model consists of two main ingredients: those that are 'important' and those that are 'urgent.' Let us have another look at these concepts.

Important

Important things are things connected with your values and motives (see 2.6). For example, if to you 'creativity' and 'being practically-oriented' are important, it is logical to give more attention to practical and creative assignments. But equally important are activities contributing to your personal targets (see proceeding sections) and your highest priorities. Maybe your main target is to become a marketing manager later in life because you love marketing as a profession. In that case you will find marketing subjects important because they are related to your target. Then the training of marketing skills will also become important. This means that to you marketing and marketing skills will have a higher priority than other subjects. That is, of course, if it is really the target you are aiming at.

Urgent

Urgent things are things requiring attention quickly. They have to happen *now* and not a second later, suggesting a shortage of time. Somebody wants an answer *now*. Your teacher wants to see your paper *today*. Sometimes something is both urgent and important: it has to be done now *and* it is related to your targets. For example, this can happen when that paper deals with your core subject and you definitely want to pass. But sometimes something is urgent but unimportant: the thing that has to happen *now* won't help you reach your targets at all! For example, somebody needs your help with a mathematical problem *now*, while you would prefer to study for an important exam.

Setting priorities

How do you avoid being saddled with lots of urgent matters that are not really important? And how do you see to it that you have enough time for important matters? Simple. Setting priorities. This means doing the most important things first and not at the very end. You will therefore postpone the least important items. This is a matter of planning your work but even more so of daring to make clear-cut choices. We have to try to be a 'planner.' But according to Sean Covey (2005) we often fail in that: often we are procrastinators, yes-men or wasters.

Procrastinators

Procrastinators postpone and postpone... and then have to perform under immense pressure. Consequently they have a problem: they are deluged by things that are both urgent and important. No wonder that they have hardly any control over those things. This happens to everybody occasionally: if your best friend has just had an accident it is an urgent and important matter to take him or her to the hospital. Other matters will just have to wait. But sometimes it may be your own fault: for example, if you have been putting off doing your homework for some time and then sit down to study the evening before the test. When it is an important test this is particularly unfortunate, because now, along with a shortage of time, there is the risk that you will not pass the test. People who often do those things tend to suffer from stress. They constantly find themselves having to perform under high pressure and lose all track of the situation. Furthermore, their results are likely to be only average: everything is done in a great hurry and nothing is done properly.

Yes-men

Yes-men say 'yes' to everything and do not concentrate on important matters. Everything they do has a sense of urgency, though nothing is important. They do not say 'no' when someone drops by, not even when they are just planning to write an important chapter. They do not say 'no' to extra work, not even when they do not really have the time because they have an important test coming up. They do not say 'no' to friends who want to go to the pub while they have an interview for an internship the next day. And they say 'yes' to each proposal without checking whether it fits their own targets and priorities. Of course, all of us sometimes say 'yes' too often. But if you do so too often, you will lose sight of what is really important to you.

Wasters

Wasters are perpetrators of activities that are neither urgent nor important. They sleep in for hours, surf the Internet for nights on end, spend hours in front of the television, are on their mobiles continuously and probably drink far too much. Sometimes a bit of letting go can be quite healthy: no urgent or important things for awhile, wonderful! But when you overdo it, nothing that you do is urgent or important. You are simply wasting your time. And suddenly you will not have any time left for the things that are really important.

Planners

All the types described above fail to pay enough attention to what is important because they do not set any priorities. Planners do not have that problem. They are mainly occupied with matters which are important but not urgent. They avoid having a shortage of time by planning ahead. Suppose a planner knows he has to go for an internship in six months' time and that he will have to find that spot. He realises that the internship must suit his personal values (e.g. being practically-oriented and creative) and his personal target (e.g. gaining experience in marketing management). Consequently he starts his search *now* and not in five or six months' time. In this way he avoids running out of time and thereby increases his chances of finding a good place for an internship. Important targets often seem far away, making it very tempting to postpone things. But only the planner will have enough time for those things which he finds really important.

Priorities

This is why he sets priorities: the most important things come first and the least important things come last. Planners often make a

Week plan

week plan: each week they take about a quarter of an hour to put things in order. They often also draw up a to-do list: a list of things that will have to be done on a specific day. Simple tools, but very effective!

Assignment 3.14 What type am I?
Sometimes everybody is a procrastinator, yes-man, waster or planner. But in which type do you recognise yourself most? And what are the consequences for you?
a Give two recent examples of things you have postponed. Was the postponement appropriate or not? Are you something of a procrastinator, or not at all? Explain.
b Give two examples (preferably recent) of situations in which you agreed to something but should not have, thereby not meeting your priorities. Why did you say yes? What would you do differently next time? And are you really a yes-man or not? Explain.
c Give two recent examples of wasting time (such as watching television or pub crawling). Was it still healthy relaxation or was it really a waste of your time? Are you really a time waster or not? Explain.
d Give two examples (preferably recent) of really planning important things properly. Which priorities – i.e. important matters first – did you set? Why did you find those things important? Are you a real planner or is there still plenty of room for improvement? Explain.

Assignment 3.15 Establishing priorities
This assignment is intended to help you become a better planner. Think of your main personal targets (see Section 3.7) and your personal values and motives (see Section 2.6). Then start formulating your priorities. To start with:

a Name the two most important specific targets you want to attain within the long or medium long term (a minimum of about four weeks). Some things you could consider are exams, finding a place for an internship, extra work on certain competencies, and so on. Explain why these are your priorities and not other things.

b Set up a time schedule. Indicate what action you will take and when to meet these specific targets.

c Discuss these priorities with your teacher or tutor and also discuss the time schedule.

Assignment 3.16 Planning your week

This assignment is also designed to help you become a better planner. In the preceding assignment we talked about long-term targets. But these are not the only ones. Real planners take a quarter of an hour each week to make a list of all the things that still have to be done. This is a case of setting priorities as well: the most important things come first.

a At the beginning of the week, set aside 15 or 20 minutes before you actually start work. Make up your mind to only plan large chunks of time: only the things that are important and will take some time to do.

b Ask yourself 'what are the most important things I have to do this week?' Indicate why these things have priority (in connection with long-term targets, personal targets, and so on). Write down the things you have to do for your studies as well as extracurricular things that you find important.

c If necessary, also write down the tasks for that week (e.g. acting as chairperson or minutes secretary, or a task you have taken on for a certain project).

d Provide an estimate of the time you will need for all these things. Tip: do not plan more than ten to fifteen of these activities. But do not curtail yourself because then you will not attain the maximum result.

e Evaluate what you have done at the end of the week. Have you reached your targets or not? If not, what was the reason?

3.10 The Deming Cycle: plan, do, check, act!

In the preceding section we saw that planning and setting priorities are important in attaining your targets. But more is needed: you will have to execute your plans. This means you must plan your actions and also check them. This is very important because in practice, plans often need to be modified. Even professionals regularly modify their planned actions in order to attain their targets. You will have to do the same.

Control cycle

You could use a fairly simple control cycle. In it you check:
· What happens (your actions, results, etc.)
· What should happen (your targets, planned actions)
· What needs to be adjusted to get closer to your targets, or maybe what should be adjusted in the targets themselves.

What you are in fact doing is looking at the real situation, at the desired situation, and at adjustments needed to move the real situation closer to the desired situation.

PDCA cycle

You should therefore set clear targets and keep checking whether you have reached them. To make sure you are on track, we advise you to use Deming's PDCA cycle, which consists of the steps 'plan,' 'do,' 'check,' and 'act'.

- *Plan* Ask yourself 'what do I *want* to do, and within what time frame?' Before you start working, identify the *desired situation*. That is, set clear targets and clearly indicate what you need to do to reach those targets. For that we advise you to use the four-step method from Section 6.1. Make your targets specific, divisible, measurable and attainable. Targets that are too vague or not measurable cannot be checked.
- *Do* Carry out your plans and even more importantly, closely monitor what you are doing. Just write down the hours spent and the results. Ask yourself: 'what am I *actually* doing and how much time is it taking?' For example, today I read ten pages in an hour. Monitoring of this sort will keep you in touch with the *real situation*. You will be keeping a close tab on what you actually do and how long you take about it.
- *Check* Ask yourself: '*How* am I doing it, and is it still going according to my planning?' Compare what you are actually doing (and how long it takes) with what you had planned. In other words, compare the desired situation (targets and planning) with the real situation (execution).
- *Act* Ask yourself: 'What do I *have to do* to improve?' As soon as you realise there are obvious differences between the desired situation and the real situation it is time to make adjustments. Most of the time you will have to adjust your actions, set other priorities, make an extra effort, and so on. But you may also have to adjust your target. Note that you must check these adjustments again using the PDCA cycle!

An example: in four weeks time you want to have finished reading a book of twelve chapters. You had planned to read three chapters each week and you think you will need an hour per chapter ('plan'). In week 1 you record what you are doing. You actually do invest three hours (an hour each day) but you finish only one and a half chapters ('do'). You compare what you have done with what you had planned and realise that 'I am only reaching half of what I want to reach'. You also note that it is not really efficient to read for only one hour. In such a time you cannot properly concentrate ('check'). Next, you plan ways of improving things: each week you will spend six hours reading. But you will also raise your efficiency and concentration: not an hour per session but three hours twice a week and fully concentrated ('act'). This is an adjusted time schedule (a new plan) and you should check this, too, using the PDCA cycle.

Note: you should finish all parts of this cycle properly, or otherwise fall short of the task in terms of your self-control and self-management. If you have no clear targets or planning, your so-called plan will disappear and there will be nothing to check. If you do not check what you are actually doing ('do') you will not be checking anything. If you do not check whether you are keeping to your schedule ('check') you will lose control of what you are doing. And if you do things haphazardly ('act'), all previous checks will be a complete waste of time. In brief: if you really want to reach something you have to follow the PDCA cycle!

Assignment 3.17 Implementing the PDCA cycle

You can combine this assignment with Assignment 3.16, which is about planning your week. The following assignment goes a bit further: you will go through the complete PDCA cycle. Do that as follows:

Plan

a *Plan* Choose a target that is important to you and which you want to reach within a number of weeks (a certain competency you want to master by then, writing a paper, doing an exam) and formulate clear objectives. In doing this, follow the four-step method as explained in Section 6.1.

Do

b *Do* Regularly check what you accomplish and in how much time. Suggestion: set up a timetable showing the hours spent and the results attained. Update this table daily.

Check

c *Check* Check at least once a week whether you are on schedule. Compare your targets with your specific activities and intermediate results.

Act

d *Act* Write down all deviations from your targets and planning and formulate adjustments. These adjustments will have to be checked again using the PDCA cycle.

e Evaluate the full PDCA cycle. Did you actually reach your targets (the original and/or the modified)? What deviations did you note during the process ('check')? What modifications had to be made ('act')? How effective were they? Do you think you have demonstrated that you have now mastered the PDCA cycle? If so, in what way exactly? If not, what can you do about it?

f Record all parts of this assignment in writing or in your PDP Toolbox. Discuss them with your teacher.

Assignment 3.18 Learning from your mistakes using the PDCA cycle

There is nothing wrong with making mistakes as long as you learn from them. Investigate at least one recent situation in which you did not attain certain results. Use the PDCA cycle to find out what you could have done differently and also what you may be able to improve.

a First, give a brief description of the situation. What exactly did you want to attain and how important was that? What are the consequences of your not having attained this specific target?

b How good was the 'plan' part? In other words, what were the targets and were they clear enough? Check that using the four-step method from Section 6.1. Were the targets specific, divisible, measurable and attainable?

c How about the 'do'? How did you check your progress? Did you check it properly?

d How was the 'check'? Did you keep an accurate record of whether you were on schedule? Did you check often enough that you were doing enough and were doing it correctly? Which criteria did you apply?

e How did the 'act' go? Did you decide to go about certain parts differently (e.g. spend more hours or plan the hours differently?) Or did you reformulate your targets?

f Look at all the foregoing aspects and indicate what could have been improved in this cycle. Give examples of improvements you could make in respect of all four parts of the PDCA cycle. Draw up a new PDCA cycle on the basis of this and, if necessary, implement it to reach the target after all. If the latter is not viable, draw up a new PDCA cycle for another important target (see the preceding assignment).

g Present all the answers from above to your teacher and discuss the progress of your PDCA cycle with him or her.

3.11   Contact with interns

An internship is important to competency management since that is where you will gain your first important practical experience. This practical experience is important for questions such as 'What can I do already?', 'What do I still have to do?' and 'What do I want to become?' It is reason enough to prepare fully for the experience! The next assignment is intended to help you with that. Shortly before you start an internship, you will interview interns or ex-interns to learn from their experiences.

Assignment 3.19 Interviewing an intern

a Form pairs and interview two students from your school who have recently completed their internship. Prepare the interview thoroughly by first making a list of questions and presenting this list to your teacher. Consult Section 6.6, The interview.
Keep on asking questions: ask the interviewee for as many examples as possible, because otherwise their story will not be sufficiently clear. Make sure to ask the following questions:
  · What was their most important learning experience (what did they find most instructive and interesting)?
  · What is their final judgement (are they satisfied about their internship or not, and why)?
  · What were their study targets?
    – What were their study targets when they started the internship?
    – Did they reach those targets? How?
  · What were the differences and similarities between 'school' and 'internship'?
    – How did their working day compare to a day at school?
    – What are the differences between school theory and internship experiences?
    – Which courses were useful in relation to their internship?
  · What tips do you regard as being most important?

b Based on this, make a report with a clear beginning and ending. Do not quote literally what the interviewees have said, but summarise in your own words. At the end, clearly indicate the conclusions you have drawn from the interview. Make sure you indicate what you have learned from the interview. Also indicate what you expect from the internship after the interview.

 Enter your list of questions and the report of the interview in the Assignments section of your PDP Toolbox.

3.12 Your own internship

For a successful internship, you need to prepare yourself well. This assignment, just as the previous one, is meant as preparation for your internship. But this one is meant mainly to get you thinking before you start. You could discuss the results of this assignment with your teacher or tutor, and with the mentor in the company or institution where your internship will take place. If you do so, you will be well prepared for your internship.

Assignment 3.20 Preparation for your internship

a Indicate your four strongest and your two weakest points and illustrate them with examples. You may use results from former assignments in this chapter.
b Indicate how you propose to use those strong points in your internship.
c What do you expect to learn in this internship? List your main study targets (see Section 6.1) and explain why you have chosen them. Describe briefly how you propose to attain these targets (i.e. which list of action points you will plan for yourself).
d What appeals to you most about your forthcoming internship?
e What problems do you foresee?
f What do you expect from the supervision? How intensive should the supervision be, in which areas would you like support, and in which way do you want to be supported?

 On the basis of the answer to *a* update your personality profile in the PDP Toolbox.
Write a report of the answers of *b, d, e* and *f* in your PDP Toolbox in the Assignments section. Enter the action points of *c* in the section PDP Action Points and Logbook.

3.13 A learning work experience

You should look back on a period in which you had a work-related learning experience – an internship or a project – and assess your own performance. This will give you a better understanding of the questions 'What can I do already?', 'What do I want to become?' and

'Where do I fit in?' Your associates will often have a different view of your strengths and weaknesses than you do. This is why during an internship you should ask for feedback from colleagues and your supervisor in the company or institution of your internship. Ask for feedback from your fellow students or your tutor during projects. Put simply: ask them regularly what you are doing right and what you are doing wrong. Ask for specific examples: 'you are quite flexible' does not mean much if no example is given.

The next assignment is for second and third year students. Do this assignment at the end of an internship. But it is also useful at the end of a project, or at the end of term. It is advisable, therefore, to do this assignment several times. Discuss this with your teacher.

You could combine the assignment with an interview (see Section 6.6 The interview). What exactly are the qualities needed for positions that you find interesting? What is your company's *modus operandi*? Consult experts! You can also combine the assignment with your action points and logbook (see Section 6.2). Check your study targets during the entire internship or project. Consult your teacher about this.

Assignment 3.21 Self-assessment after a work-related learning experience

In your self-assessment pay attention to the following (you do not have to adhere strictly to this sequence):

a Indicate briefly what your study targets were when you started this internship or project. Also indicate which study targets you met and which ones you did not. Explain using specific examples if possible.

b Describe at least five situations on the shop floor in which you think you performed well. Do not make the mistake of assuming that you did not accomplish anything; simply describe events that you look back on with satisfaction. Also ask your tutor or another colleague to mention situations in which you performed well according to him/her, and ask him/her for comment (i.e. feedback) for the examples you have given yourself. You will find tips about receiving feedback in Section 6.4.
   · Describe the situation accurately but briefly.
   · Which specific things did you undertake? ('Making proposals' is an action too.)
   · Which skills and/or competencies did you show in this situation? (Consult your study profile.)
   · What exactly was the result? How was what you did received? What reactions were there to your proposal or action? Was your tutor also satisfied about what you did and/or said, and why?

c Briefly describe at least two situations on the shop floor in which you performed less well. In doing so, pay attention to the following:
   · Here, too, describe the situation accurately but briefly.
   · Ask your tutor or another colleague to comment on (i.e. give feedback) examples that come to you and to provide some examples of their own.

- Try to indicate which 'points for improvement' or 'weak points' prevented success in this case (i.e. list which of your skills proved inadequate).
- Indicate specifically what you would do differently the next time (and also how).

d Indicate what you think are your strongest and weakest points and illustrate these with specific examples. They can be the situations described under b and c, but not necessarily so.

e Now provide an answer (based on a, b, c and d) to the question What can I do? This will boil down to a brief conclusion concerning your strengths and weaknesses.

f Next, deal with the questions 'What do I want to do?' and 'Where do I fit in?' These questions primarily concern the profession which you (also taking into account this work experience) find most appealing.

g When answering f also deal with your competencies: review the competencies of the study and briefly indicate which competency (at least one) you find useful and which (at least one) does not. Be succinct.

h State your core motive. A core motive is what specifically satisfies someone, and what he will always consciously or subconsciously strive for in his work. This also includes your future work and this internship!

i Somewhere in the report write down the study targets you had before, during and after this period. Those study targets must tie in with the questions 'What can I do already?', 'What do I want to become?' and 'Where do I fit in?' For this, follow Section 6.1. Study these targets with particular reference to the weak points you will have to improve upon in relation to the sort of profession you are striving for (see b to e above).

 On the basis of this assignment update your personality profile in the PDP Toolbox. Make a report of this assignment in your PDP Toolbox in the Assignments section.

3.14 Motivation and development

In managing your competencies, it is important to ask yourself on a regular basis what your motivation is. It is also important to do this during your studies. Are you on the right track? And what is that track? What is your target and are you aiming to reach it? It is a good idea to check your knowledge, skills and attitude; as you know, these are the three building blocks of competencies.

Assignment 3.22 My motivation

a What is your main motive in continuing your studies? What do you want to achieve? Name at least two targets. Mention what you find specifically interesting about your studies, your future profession or the kind of work you want to do later. A target such as 'getting my diploma' is too obvious and does not count as an answer! The same goes for 'It's what my parents want' – that is not *your* motivation!

b   Which subjects or areas (themes, projects) up until now were the most useful or interesting? Why? Link your answers up with your answers to question *a*: if you know which areas were most interesting to you and why, you will already have an understanding of your motivation!

c   Describe the main skills you have learned or those you have developed really well at school up until now. Explain and give examples in which those skills are clearly demonstrated.

d   What is the most important area of knowledge you have mastered so far? Explain and give examples clearly showing you have indeed mastered that knowledge.

e   Which aspects in a particular field of knowledge and skills deserve extra attention? In other words, which weaknesses do you want to rectify? Why? How?

f   Who motivates you to continue your studies (think of students, teachers, members of your family)? Indicate what they do specifically to motivate you and in what way they succeed.

 Make a report of the second assignment in your PDP Toolbox in the Assignments section.

3.15   Higher education thinking and working level: ten generic core qualifications

Core qualifications

For many vacancies, a specific educational course is not called for but rather a 'higher education thinking and working level'. What is that exactly? In the Netherlands, some years ago the Netherlands Association of Universities of Professional Education formulated the so-called generic core qualifications (see Table 3.1). These qualifications are used to determine whether a course of education is actually at the level it purports to be at. In this assignment you will use these qualifications to determine your own higher education level. This is not difficult: these core qualities indicate competencies that may be expected from all students at a higher education level.

Assignment 3.23 Testing your core qualities
a   Study the ten generic core qualities in Table 3.1.

b   For each separate quality enter a score for yourself: 'good', 'sufficient', 'poor' or 'insufficient'.

c   Briefly explain each score, preferably referring to specific examples. Suppose you score 'good' for quality 6, 'Problem-orientated working', which relates to 'independently defining and analysing complex problem situations based on relevant information'. Then use examples to show that you have done well on a few occasions.

d   Indicate your follow-up strategy. Therefore:
   · First say whether you are satisfied with your total score or not, and provide arguments.

Table 3.1 **Ten higher education core qualities according to the Netherlands Association of Universities of Professional Education**

Ten higher education core qualities

1 **Developing as a professional** The student shows clear evidence of familiarity with current insights, concepts and research results of a scientific nature (in the broadest sense) as well as with developments (national and international) in the sphere of employment as outlined in the professional profile and in order to be able to:
   a Independently execute the tasks of a starting professional
   b Function within a work organization
   c Advance within in the chosen profession
2 **Multidisciplinary integration** There is clear evidence of an ability to be able to integrate information, insights, attitudes and skills (relating to various job disciplines) from the perspective of professional conduct.
3 **Scientific application** There is clear evidence of an ability to apply available relevant insights, theories, concepts and research results of a scientific nature (in the broadest sense) to those issues that graduates face as they embark on their career.
4 **Transfer and wider employability** There is clear evidence of an ability to apply information, insights and skills to various occupational situations.
5 **Creativity and complexity** There is clear evidence of an ability to tackle work-related matters in which the problem is not clearly delineated in advance and to which the standard procedures are not applicable.
6 **Problem-oriented work approaches** There is clear evidence of an ability to independently define and analyze complex and problematical situations based on relevant information and insights (both theoretical and practical), to apply meaningful problem-solving strategies (both new and existing) and to judge their efficacy.
7 **Methodical and reflective thinking and action-taking** There is clear evidence of an ability to set realistic targets, plan activities and reflect on both individual approaches as well as those of a professional nature based on the gathering and analysis of relevant information.
8 **Socio-communicative skills** There is clear evidence of an ability to communicate and cooperate with others in a multicultural, international and/or multidisciplinary environment and to meet the demands of participation in a work environment.
9 **Basic qualifications for management functions** There is clear evidence of an ability to perform simple executive and managerial tasks.
10 **Awareness of social responsibility** There is an understanding and engagement in relation to ethical, normative and social questions in conjunction with the application of knowledge and current and future vocational practice.

- What is your choice: concentrating on your strong points, or improving your weak ones? Provide arguments, and indicate how this ties in with your future profession.
- Indicate your study targets and work out at least one in a plan of progressing steps. Consult Section 6.1, Study targets, in four steps.

 Make a report of *a, b* and *c* in your PDP Toolbox in the Assignments section.

Enter the study targets you have found in working out *d* as action points in the PDP Action points section and logbook of the PDP Toolbox.

3.16   Higher education thinking and working level: the Dublin descriptors

In 3.15 we pointed out the following: people often ask for a 'higher education thinking and working level'. This level can be measured (as we have seen) using the ten generic core qualifications. However, the 'Dublin descriptors' have become more prominent in recent times. These descriptors describe the final level and final qualifications of various kinds of studies, such as bachelor's and master's degrees. The Dublin descriptors were defined in Dublin in 2004 and aimed to be able to compare the levels of schooling in different countries.

The Dublin descriptors address questions such as the following: Do I have enough knowledge and understanding? How good am I at implementing them? How sound is my judgement? How good are my communicative skills? How strong is my learning capacity? These are all questions that are relevant to competency management. This is why it is advisable to check regularly whether your competencies do indeed comply with the Dublin descriptors. It is advisable to repeat the following assignment a few times.

Assignment 3.24 Testing your Dublin descriptors
a   Study the Dublin descriptors in Table 3.2.
b   For each row of this table – so for each descriptor – write down your specific situation. This equates to giving:
   · A score ('excellent', 'good', 'adequate', or 'poor')
   · Arguments, examples and any evidence to justify the score.
c   State your follow-up strategy. Therefore:
   · First say whether or not you are satisfied with your overall score and provide reasons.
   · What choices do you have: further reinforce your strong points or improve the weak points? Explain.
   · State your study targets and draw up a step-by-step plan accordingly. See Section 6.1, Study targets in four steps.

Enter a report of a, b, and c in your PDP Toolbox in the Assignments section.

Table 3.2 **Dublin descriptors**

Knowledge and understanding	Applying knowledge and understanding	Making judgements	Communication	Learning skills
Has demonstrable knowledge and understanding of a professional domain which is an amelioration of the level reached in higher education and supersedes it.	Usually functions at a level where with the support of specialised manuals some aspects arise for which knowledge of the latest developments in the professional domain is needed. Is capable of applying his/her knowledge and understanding in such a way that it shows a professional approach to his/her profession. Also possesses competencies in setting up and refining lines of reasoning and for the solving of problems in the professional domain.	Is capable of gathering and interpreting relevant data (most often in the professional domain) in order to arrive at a judgement which is also based on the consideration of relevant sociological, scientific or ethical aspects.	Is capable of communicating in formation, ideas and solutions to an audience consisting of specialists or non specialists.	Possesses the learning skills needed to complete a follow-up study presupposing a high level of autonomy.

3.17 My personality profile

After you have gathered sufficient information about your capabilities, ambitions and personal traits, it is time to set up a personality profile. In it, you will state briefly but clearly what you can and want to do. Write down your strong sides, explain under which circumstances you perform best, and also which functions and type of organization appeal to you most. In brief, provide a succinct answer to the by now familiar questions 'Who am I?', 'What do I want to do?', 'What can I do?' and 'Where do I fit in?' It is advisable to set up a personality profile regularly throughout your studies; in the beginning, somewhere half-way, and towards the end. Managing your competencies also means tracking your own development, and that you can do by making a record several times in a personality profile of 'where you stand'.

View the profile as a kind of database for letters of application, job interviews and your curriculum vitae. You will set up the personality profile for your benefit only, as against always directing a letter of application and your CV to a reader (see Sections 6.8 and 6.9). For each application, consult your personality profile. The profile should not be too long; one or two pages will suffice.

An important tip: strive to be concise and clear! For example, 'I am a good organiser' is too vague: provide an explanation and specific examples. What exactly do you mean by 'organise'? What kind of things have you organised? You must be able to promote your strong points especially; after all, these are the points that distinguish you from the rest of the applicants. During a job interview, how can you convince someone of your organisational talents? The best way is by using examples and by explaining. It is better to say: 'I am good at organising events. For the past two years I have organised well-run excursions for logistics students. I took care of the advertising and catering, and saw to it that others organised speakers. I was appointed head coordinator and therefore bore final responsibility.'

Parts of your personality profile

The personality profile contains the following parts:

- *What can I do? Experience.* Briefly describe your training and experience. Also indicate the areas of knowledge you are familiar with (for example, refer to the courses that have meant most to you) and areas in which you are really experienced. Also mention part-time jobs and the like.
- *What can I do? Strong points: qualities, skills, competencies.* Describe your main qualities, i.e. those skills and qualities you are certain that you possess. To reiterate, be specific and clear! Write down your strong points in such a way that later (with applications) they will be very persuasive!
- *Points for improvement and points requiring attention.* Describe your points for improvement: for example, indicate situations in which you are prone to attracting criticism. Of course, you should not write this in a CV, but in job interviews you will invariably be questioned in this regard and consequently it should be part of your personality profile. Also indicate briefly how you are addressing these points. Do you need to modify your behavior and if so, how do you intend to go about this?
- *What do I want to do? Where do I fit in?* At this point you can deal with the following questions, but you do not have to answer all of them. Choose what you think are the most important questions. You might also think of other points requiring attention. Suggestions: Under which circumstances do you perform best? What kind of work is most satisfying to you? Do you prefer to work in a group or by yourself? What do you prefer: a clear-cut assignment for which you know exactly what to do, or an 'open assignment' in which you have freedom? Are you more of a 'thinker' or a 'doer'? With all these questions think back to your internship and possible part-time jobs, or specific projects in your education.
- *My core motivation.* Everyone has a special motivation: one important aspect he will always strive for in his work. One person wants to have fun, another always wants to deliver the very best. What is your core motivation?

Assignment 3.25 Setting up the personality profile

Write your personality profile as described in this section. Guidelines for size: one or two pages.

 Enter your profile in your PDP Toolbox in the Personality Profile section.

3.18 Professional competency profile

The preceding sections have dealt with investigating your strong and weak points in various ways, and you will have taken a closer look at your performance over a given period. Hopefully, this will have given you a clearer idea of your skills. But to what extent do those skills match the competencies required by your studies and in the sphere of employment? As you know, the competencies listed in the study profile are those professional skills pertaining to a professional starting out. The question is to what degree you have attained these competencies. What will you do to reinforce your strengths and improve possible weaknesses? It is a good idea to do the following assignment several times: at the beginning of your studies, half-way through, and just before the end of your studies. By doing this assignment several times and comparing the various results you will gain a better insight into your progress.

Assignment 3.26 Setting up the professional competency profile

Make a professional competency profile. Do this as follows:
a Find the competencies required by your chosen education (in the study guide or education profile. Consult your teacher if necessary).
b List at least two competencies best suited to you and provide examples/arguments why. Examine all four aspects of competencies: knowledge, skills, attitude and behaviour (see Section 1.1). In other words, indicate what you should know and be able to do, what you want to do and what you are actually doing in respect of that competency. After that, list at least two competencies least suited to you and also provide specific examples/arguments why. Do not examine your knowledge, skills, attitude or behaviour.
c Indicate briefly with well-reasoned arguments which courses/subjects were most instructive and useful and which were least so.
d Indicate your study targets and explain why you have set them. You could choose to further develop competencies that are already well developed, or to improve 'underdeveloped' competencies. Explain your choice.
e Indicate how you will attain those study targets. To do that, consult Section 6.1. At this point, take the time to examine your knowledge, skills, attitude and behaviour. In other words, indicate here as well what you should know and be able to do, what you want to do and what you are actually doing to meet these study targets.

Enter the professional competency profile in your PDP Toolbox in the Competencies and competency profile section. Indicate if it concerns a professional competence.

Enter the results of *b* and *c* in the Assignments section.

Enter the study targets you have found in working out *d* and *e* as action points in the PDP Action points section and logbook of the PDP Toolbox.

3.19 Updating the PDP

After completing all (or at least most) of the preceding assignments, you will have answered the question 'What can I do?' many times over. Your answers will also have varied assignments in which you review a work-related learning experience may yield different insights to assignments in which you utilise the MDI behaviour theory or in assignments on time management. It is useful to compare the various results and to get a complete picture.

After reading Chapter 2 you will have made a PDP in the Toolbox based on assignments concerning the question 'Who am I?' In all those assignments the emphasis was on personality traits and attitude. In the following assignments you will refer to the PDP based on the assignments in Chapter 3. The emphasis is now more on individual skills, i.e. on the question 'What can I do as an individual?'

Assignment 3.27 Updating your personality profile
Begin by reading through all the reports you made of the assignments in this chapter. Proceed to the Personality Profile section of the PDP Toolbox and fill in as much as possible on the basis of the completed assignments.

Assignment 3.28 Updating your competencies
During your studies you will discover which competencies you need for your future profession and you will also acquire more competencies.

Regularly enter your new and acquired competencies in the Competencies and Competency profile in your PDP Toolbox.

What can I do in a team?

In the previous chapter you will have investigated your competencies as an individual. In this chapter we deal with competencies in working within a group. The first two sections contain group assessments in which the performance of the group as a whole and the performance of each individual group member are investigated. Assignment 4.1 (to be done several times) is intended for first year students; assignment 4.2 for advanced students. The group assessment described in Section 4.3 relates to competencies that are central to the project.

Section 4.4 concerns a group assessment using the 'Belbin test'. The following sections concern which type of team role (and style of behaviour) suits you best. Each time, however, the approach varies slightly, so that the assignments do not overlap.

In the final assignment we ask you to complete an overall view of yourself as a team worker.

4.1 Group assessment

The next assignment will be carried out in the first year. You will do this during school projects in which you work with fellow students on a practical assignment. Together with your team members you will investigate the strengths and weaknesses of the group, and the strengths and weaknesses of each individual, yourself included.

This type of assessment also occurs in the sphere of employment and so it is useful to do this during your studies. You will also learn to give and receive feedback, which is an important professional skill. However, the most important thing is to receive feedback on your functioning within the group. This is important for your PDP, and consequently for managing your competencies.

You will complete Assignment 4.1 during your first and second study projects (possibly also your third), together with your fellow students. This means you will do this assignment two or three times but it does not mean doing the same thing twice. Project groups and projects are never identical, so you will not function in exactly the same manner twice. During the work, you will determine what has gone well and what needs improving. This you will discuss with your fellow students (who are also doing this assignment). Then you will receive and give feedback. Between assignments, you will determine what is going well and what can be improved on. Next, you will discuss these things with your fellow students who will have done the same assignment. Since this is the first time you and your fellow students will have done this assignment, we have included a checklist as a tool in Appendix 3.

Assignment 4.1 Evaluating a group

Part 1 Preparation
Do the following assignments and present the results to your tutor. He will assist in the assessment discussion later. Keep your own copies of the results and take these along for the assessment discussion.

1a Self-evaluation
- Fill in the self-evaluation checklist (see Appendix 3). For each proposition circle your score. Do not forget the total score.
- Give an explanation and examples of at least two significant scores in the self-evaluation (e.g. the highest and lowest score).
- Then, briefly indicate your best points and provide an explanation. You may refer to the checklist but you can also bring up other points.
- Briefly indicate at least one of your weaker points, one that you would like to improve upon (supplying a brief explanation). You may refer to the self-evaluation, but you can also bring up other points.

1b Group assessment and group members evaluation
- Fill in the checklist, Evaluation of group members (see Appendix 4) for each of your fellow group members. For each proposition circle the score you feel your fellow group members deserve. Again, do not forget the total score.

Then answer the following questions:
- What are the strongest points of this group? In other words, what went really well? Please provide a brief explanation.
- What could or must be improved upon in this group? In other words, what is not going well? Please provide a brief explanation.
- What is your final evaluation of the group? Indicate the extent to which the group possesses information and skills, and what information and/or skills need improving.

Part 2 The assessment discussion

With the tutor as chairman, discuss the evaluation with the whole group. Duration: one lecture hour. Discuss the following points:
- What went well in the group, and what not so well? What is the final evaluation? What specifically must the group improve upon, and how?
- What does each individual do well, and what not so well? What is the average total score? What specifically must be improved upon, and how? Pay attention to the check list scores and the average total score for each individual student.

The minutes secretary will record all strengths and weaknesses of the group as a whole, and of each individual group member. He will also record the final evaluations. Furthermore, he will record the agreements on how the group (and each individual group member) plans to tackle the points for improvement. These minutes will serve as a piece of evidence for your portfolio.

A few tips for this discussion:
- Always start with the good points and never lose sight of them.
- Everyone makes mistakes; it does not matter if points for improvement are identified.
- Things that are never discussed will never be improved.
- Everyone must take an active part in the assessment discussions.
- Be mindful of the rules for giving and receiving feedback. Consult Sections 6.3 and 6.4 for this.

Part 3 Subsequent individual reflection

Within a week of the assessment, provide a detailed written response to the following questions (present your findings to the tutor in question):
- Prior to the assessment discussion, what did you consider to be your strong and weak points?
- Which strong and weak points did others recognise in you and mention in the assessment discussion?
- How did the feedback on your performance tally (or not) with what you had established yourself? Also indicate whether you agree with the feedback (both the positive and the more critical).
- Which points do you plan to improve? Why? How?

Part 4 Final assessment
Parts 1 to 3 were all concerned with intermediate evaluations halfway through the project. But for the final assessment, the final evaluation at the end of the project is, of course, crucial. The assignment is as follows:

4a Self-assessment
- Assess yourself again. To do so, follow the instructions in Part 1 (1a Self-assessment) above.
- Briefly indicate what has improved or changed in any way since the intermediate evaluation.

4b Group members
Once again, assess the group and its members. To do so, follow the instructions in part 1 (1b Group assessment and group member assessment) above, in which the assessment of the group members is especially important.

After consulting you, the teacher may decide to have another assessment talk, following the same procedure as in Part 2 above. However, this is not strictly necessary.

 Enter the results of parts 1, 2, 3 and 4 of this assignment in your PDP Toolbox in the Assignments section. You can make a printout of these via the Toolbox.
Also update your Personality Profile regarding your weak and strong points.
Enter the points for improvement you have identified in Part 3 as action points under the PDP Action Points section and in the logbook of the PDP Toolbox.

4.2 Group assessment for advanced students

Together with your fellow students, halfway through a study project in the second year of your studies or later, do the assignment in this section. You should determine what went well and what could be improved. Discuss these matters with your fellow students (those who will also be carrying out the assignment). In doing so, you will receive and give feedback. There are many similarities with Assignment 4.1, the difference being that more tools were provided for the earlier assignment. As an advanced student you no longer need so many.

Assignment 4.2 Evaluating a group of advanced students

Part 1 Preparation
Do the following assignments in writing, and present the results to your tutor. He will assist in the assessment discussion later. Keep your own copies of the results and take these along for the assessment discussion.
- Indicate your stronger and weaker points and specify at least two of each. Restrict yourself to your functioning within the group.

Decide whether you possess the required information and skills for this project and illustrate all these points (the strong and weaker ones) with examples. Also, indicate specifically how you could improve the weakest ones.

- Indicate the two strongest and the two weakest points of the group and briefly explain with examples. Also, give an overall assessment after taking into consideration the strong and weak points; i.e. does the group function well or not? Does the group possess the required information and skills? Give reasons for your assessment.
- Specify the two strongest and the two weakest points of each group member and explain briefly (with examples, if possible). Always supply the first name and surname of the group member concerned. For each group member also give your overall assessment: for example, 'good group member', 'average group member', 'poor group member', 'the strong points outweigh the weaker ones', and so on.

Part 2 The evaluation discussion

With the tutor as chairman, discuss the evaluation with the full group. Duration: one or two lecture hours. Discuss the following points:

- What went well in the group, and what not so well? What is the overall assessment? What must the group specifically improve on, and how?
- What does each individual do well, and what not so well? What is the overall assessment? What must each member specifically improve, and how?

The minutes secretary will record all of the strengths and weaknesses of the group as a whole, and of each individual group member. He will also record the overall assessments. Furthermore, he will record the agreements on how the group (and each individual group member) plans to tackle the points for improvement. Once again, these minutes will serve as a piece of evidence in your portfolio.

A few tips for this discussion:

- Always start with the good points and never lose sight of them.
- Everyone makes mistakes; it does not matter if points for improvement are identified.
- Things that are not discussed will not be improved.
- Everyone must take an active part in the assessment discussions.
- Be mindful of the rules for giving and receiving feedback in appendices 6.3 and 6.4.

Part 3 Subsequent individual reflection

Within a week of the assessment, provide a detailed written response to the following questions (present this to the tutor concerned):

- Prior to the assessment discussion, what did you consider to be your strong and weaker points?
- Which strong and weaker points did others recognise in you and mention in the assessment discussion?

- How did the feedback on your performance tally (or not) with what you yourself thought? Also indicate whether you agree with the feedback (both the positive and the more critical).
- Which points do you plan to improve? Why? How?

Part 4 Final assessment

Parts 1 to 3 were all concerned with intermediate evaluations halfway through the project. But of course, for the final assessment, the final evaluation at the end of the project is important. The assignment is as follows:

4a Self-assessment
- Assess yourself again. To do so, follow the instructions in Part 1 (1a Self-assessment) above.
- Briefly indicate what has improved or changed after the intermediate evaluation.

4b Group members

Once again, assess the group and its members. To do so, follow the instructions in part 1 (1b Group assessment and group member assessment) above, in which the assessment of the group members is especially important.

After consulting you, the teacher may decide to have another assessment talk, following the same procedure as in Part 2 above. However, this is not strictly necessary.

 Enter the results of parts 1, 2, 3 and 4 of this assignment in your PDP Toolbox in the Assignments section. You can make a printout of these via the Toolbox. Also update your Personality Profile regarding your weak and strong points. Enter the points of improvement you identified in Part 3 as action points under the PDP Action Points section and in the logbook of the PDP Toolbox.

4.3   Competency-based group evaluation

In each training course or study, certain competencies are of central importance, and naturally, the members of your project team have to possess those competencies. This can only succeed if your team reflects systematically on its procedures. This is what you will do in the following assignment. You will firstly describe your competencies in your own words and then identify your targets. In subsequent intermediate assessments (that can follow the same procedure as Assignment 4.2) you will assess the group (and all its members) to ascertain whether it complies with those competencies. In the final assessment you will repeat this procedure. As you do so you should obviously work with competencies in mind. Just as with Assignment 4.2, the assessments deal with strengths and weaknesses of the group and its members. But in Assignment 4.3 these assessments focus much more on your competencies.

Assignment 4.3 Formulating competencies and assessing the group

Part 1 Initial (i.e., at the beginning of the project) enumeration and description of competencies

Firstly, enumerate the competencies which are of central importance to the project. To do so, follow the exercise book, course literature, or another source.

Reformulate and analyse these competencies in your own words. Focus on the knowledge, skills, attitude (motivation) and behaviour (professional performance plus the results) needed for the project. This means what you need to *know, be able to do, want to do* and *do* to complete this project successfully.

Based on that, set targets, a plan and a division of labour. What is the desired end result, and what is needed to reach it? Who possesses which components of these? Which competencies have to be improved, and in what way?

· Consult with your teacher and record everything in writing.

Part 2 Intermediate (midway through the project) assessment

Midway through the project assess yourself and the group members on the basis of the competencies identified in 1. Do this as follows:

· Put your strong and weak points down in writing – at least two of each. Indicate whether you think you possess enough competencies to complete this project successfully. Provide examples of your strong and weak points. Also indicate in which way you will improve specific points. Grade yourself and provide arguments for your grade.

Assess each group member in the same way. Grade each group member.

Also assess the group as a whole. Which competencies are sufficiently present, and which are not? What is already going well, and what definitely needs to be improved (and in what way?) Grade the group as well.

Based on this you will now organise an assessment talk (as in 4.1 and 4.2). Minutes of the talk should, of course, be taken.

Part 3 Final (at the end of the project) assessment

At the end of the project assess your own performance once again and the performances of your group members. To do so, follow the instructions in Part 2 above.

4.4   Group evaluation using the Belbin test

Belbin

Some project teams function perfectly, others do not. According to the organisation expert Belbin (1993) this is mainly due to the 'right mix'. He distinguishes eight character-related team roles, i.e. eight different types, each with their own character. Each type (each team role) has its own strengths and weaknesses. A good team consists of various team roles, so that the different strengths are complementary. Here follows a short description of the roles.

1   The Implementer (executive, organiser)

Characteristic quotes: 'No whining: let's go to work!' 'Let's stay focused'.

The Implementer is calm and disciplined. He is practical and quickly sees how something should be done. He is a 'worker' who never refuses an assignment, is very responsible and works systematically. He likes clarity, rhythm and regularity, and is very capable of making specific work plans. His strength lies in maintaining responsible and efficient control. The Implementer often lacks ideas, however, and is not flexible in adjusting his own plans. He is not very creative either, and often rejects new ideas. Sticking to old plans is a strong point in itself, but it makes the Implementer less open to new opportunities.
Strong points: self-control, discipline, sense of duty, realism (very quickly realises what is attainable or not), practical, systematic and efficient, common-sensical, a hard worker who takes on all tasks, organisational talent.
Weak points: not very flexible (sticks to plans too rigidly), conservative (opposes new approaches), hasty (goes to work without having investigated the background information), uncertain when goals are not clear.

2   The Plant (independent thinker, generator, person of ideas)

Characteristic quotes: 'Good ideas always seem strange', 'We must renew constantly', 'The bigger the problem, the bigger the challenge'.

The Plant is an independent creative person with original ideas whose imagination knows no bounds. He is not interested in everyday reality and routine but is particularly interested in new possibilities. He is intelligent, thinks of things no one else thinks of, and for this reason is at his best when he has a lot of freedom. He wants space to be able to create. He is dominant and radical and will choose a radically new direction without thinking things through. This can generate a lot of resistance, especially since the Plant shows little interest in practical details. Moreover, he dislikes stupidity. On the other hand, he is a constant source of inspiration and his innovative ideas are often very useful.
Strong points: intelligence, creativity, originality, knowledgeable, imaginative, developer of new ideas.
Weak points: sometimes unpractical, arrogant, ignores incidentals, ignores rules and protocols, does not analyse advantages and disadvantages properly, unclear in explaining his ideas.

3 The Resource Investigator

Characteristic quotes: 'I will find out what the problem is, I know just the right person who can help me', 'It is never wrong to get a second opinion.'

The Resource Investigator is bubbly, extrovert, enthusiastic and makes contacts easily. He is a real networker and brainstormer. He is creative: he is not good at thinking up new ideas himself, but he is good at combining different ideas into something new. He is very astute, which is why he senses new opportunities quickly. He is always looking for new stimuli and is good at improvising. He is especially alert during brainstorming sessions and extremely good at picking up on (and combining) valuable ideas. He is not very systematic, does very little preparation and, as a result, he can be chaotic. Sometimes he is too optimistic and enthusiastic, but he also becomes bored very quickly. His optimism can suddenly be deflated and he needs to be stimulated by others. Consequently, the Resource Investigator profits from activity and change.

Strong points: skilled socially, often spots new chances, challenging, always seeks and finds new ideas, creative and alert brainstormer.

Weak points: fickle, sometimes over-enthusiastic, loses interest quickly, sometimes talks too much, easily diverted, leaves others in the lurch and does not show up for appointments.

4 The Co-ordinator (process management)

Characteristic quotes: 'Delegating well is an art', 'Let us not stray from the subject'.

The Co-ordinator knows how to clarify what others mean, is good at identifying problems, encourages team members, summarises thoughts well and records decisions taken. This is how he structures the decision-making. He also oversees the 'main thrust' and formulates common goals. He is dominant in a quiet way, without being overbearing. His strength lies in stimulating creativity in others, not in generating ideas himself. He looks for consensus, but when time is short will make decisions without hesitating; has little time for in-depth discussions and does not like to revert decisions taken.

Strong points: impartial, communicative, stimulates others to contribute without losing sight of the goal, combines various talents, formulates common goals.

Weak points: not very creative, not always insightful, makes decisions too quickly (which have sometimes not been properly discussed), adheres to agreements rigidly.

5 The Shaper

Characteristic quotes: 'I am straightforward and say what I mean!', 'We have to squeeze the last drop out of it'.

The Shaper is extroverted and dynamic, is full of nervous energy, and bursting with desire to perform. He wants to win and win again. He is focused on results and insists on action. He is constantly defining priorities and goals. He is challenging, easily frustrated and impatient. He loves debates, fights and discussions. He is quick to quarrel, but forgets quickly as well. He is constantly driving others and himself. He knows how to push through important changes, even if he has to challenge the team for it. This is how he gets teams moving quickly. On the other hand, he can upset the team's balance by his drive to overcome obstacles. Many Shapers do better in a position right next to the one with the final responsibility, but prefer not to have that final responsibility themselves.

Strong points: generates action, dynamic, performance-orientated, formulates goals and priorities.

Weak points: impatient, too 'pushy', easily offends people, is provocative, quickly frustrated when things go too slowly.

6 The Monitor

Characteristic quotes: 'Let us first weigh up all the alternatives', 'Let us first think logically and investigate everything.'

The Monitor is critical, analytical, levelheaded, businesslike and not very enthusiastic. He is not very inspired. He makes decisions slowly because he wants to think about and investigate everything. He always wants to know why and explain everything first (or have it explained) before making a decision. He analyses everything, looks at things from all sides and weighs the pros and cons carefully. He is quick to spot the weak points in a plan or in the argument supporting the plan. His core qualities lie in observation, evaluating and monitoring. In complex situations these qualities are particularly valuable. He is not good in coming up with ideas (like 'the Plant'). He is not very assertive, and results are not important as long as he *understands* things.

Strong points: objectivity, critical intellect, good at analysing and evaluating, clear in his judgements.

Weak points: not a good motivator, dull and critical, prone to run things down, makes very few decisions, delays coming to a conclusion by forever finding disadvantages, reluctant to make 'gut' decisions.

7 The Completer (finisher, controller, caretaker)

Characteristic quotes: 'Has anyone checked whether this is all right?', 'Only perfect is good enough.'

The Completer is orderly, quality conscious (even a perfectionist), and has a great sense of responsibility. He is constantly checking if everything is still all right and, in doing so, he pays attention to each and every detail. He is shy but hurried as well, so that he drives others. His self-control and punctuality mean that he is always on time. He can be very stressful as well as he is constantly worried about things that can go wrong. He always takes care of unity and perfection. He also prepares everything meticulously and then works out everything according to plan. He is the quality-control champion who tests everything for reliability and quality. The Completer excels in precision and complete concentration. However, he lacks flair and opposes innovation.

Strong points: feeling for order and efficiency, meticulous and precise, a good planner, fulfils all promises and delivers the highest quality, works everything out in detail.

Weak points: too worried about details, does not delegate, intolerant towards adventurous innovations, drives himself and others into stressful situations, too focused on details and not focused enough on the 'grand design'.

8 The Team Worker

Characteristic quotes: 'Everyone has his good points and these should be put to use', 'Let's maintain a good team spirit'.

The Team Worker is strongly focused on the human side, good for the team spirit and positive towards others. He is the coach who stimulates and helps everyone. He is socially minded, mild, sensitive and very friendly. This makes the Team Worker the most supportive member of the team. He listens very attentively and gets along with everybody. Team goals are more important than his personal ones; a harmonious atmosphere is particularly important to him. He is tactful and diplomatic and good at bringing people together (also in conflict situations). He is the team builder: he sees to it that everybody gets his say and elaborates on other people's themes. This makes him a good stimulator of group feeling, but conflicts are useful sometimes, and the Team Worker prefers avoiding conflicts. Team Workers form cosy groups, without a lot of 'drive'.
Strong points: creates team spirit, a real team player, sympathetic and empathetic, flexible, serviceable, a good listener.
Weak points: too gentle (avoids conflicts that way), indecisive during differences of opinion (does not choose sides), avoids stressful situations, can become completely passive when there is no stimulus, finds it difficult to take the imitative because he is too concerned about the general atmosphere.

Assignment 4.4 Doing the Belbin test

In consultation with the teacher, combine this assignment with Assignment 4.2.

Part 1 Determine your own team role
- Find the Belbin test on the Internet (for example on www.belbin.com) and do the test. Make sure not to forget the score chart and conversion chart.
- Briefly discuss your highest scores (the three highest). Indicate briefly how those scores correspond to your behaviour in the project group. Give specific examples: for example, if you score high on 'Monitor' and you think you are good at weighing up advantages and disadvantages critically, provide an example to illustrate this.
- Briefly discuss your lowest score. According to Belbin this is a type of role that is completely unsuited to you and you should never have to fill it. Is that correct in your case?
- Give your two strongest and your two weakest points. Illustrate with examples related to your performance in the group.
- Indicate whether those strong and weak points match the results of the Belbin test. Example: someone with a high score for

'Implementer' should be good in practical matters, a real 'Shaper' is focused on performance, and so on.

Part 2 Determining the team roles of others

- Indicate for each student in your group which team role (or combination of team roles) you think suits that student best. Give a brief explanation. For example: 'I think Charlie is a Shaper because he is often very persistent and wants us to get going.'
- Indicate the two strongest and two weakest points of each student. Try to relate this to the team role they play according to you.
- Give the two strongest and two weakest points of the group as a whole. Again, try to relate this to the team roles played by your fellow students as you see it. Example: a team full of 'Implementers' and 'Shapers' is focused on results and performance, and is very practical. But because 'Resource Investigators' and 'Plants' are lacking, it is not very creative.

Part 3 Feedback and group discussion of the Belbin test

Feedback can take various forms. It depends on the situation and your teacher. Think of a lecture class, a written report by the communications teacher or a group discussion chaired by the tutor concerned. Alternatively, think of a lecture class by teacher X in combination with a group evaluation supervised by teacher Y. Decide on the form with your teacher.

Whatever the feedback form, the study targets should always be the following:

- Everyone must already have completed the test and have reflected on its results (i.e., on his team role and its strengths and weaknesses).
- Everyone must know the test results of the other group members (record these in minutes or something similar).
- Everyone must provide feedback on each other's strong and weak points.
- Everyone in the team must know what 'mix' is comprised by the team roles.
- Everyone must reflect on the team's strengths and weaknesses resulting from this mix.

Part 4 Individual reflection afterwards

The assignment is simple: after the feedback, once again write down your strongest and weakest points, and indicate how these correspond to the team roles of the Belbin test. In relation to this, discuss the following:

- The feedback of your fellow students (which role they had assigned to you and, according to them, what your strengths and weaknesses are)
- Your study targets (which things you want to improve and how you plan to go about that)

 Enter the reports of part 1, 2, 3 and 4 of this assignment in your PDP Toolbox in the Assignments section. Also update your Personality

Profile concerning the weak and strong points you have according to the Belbin roles and those which you see yourself as having in reality. Enter the study targets and points for improvement you have found in part 4 as action points in the PDP Action Points section and logbook of the PDP Toolbox.

4.5 Group roles

This section deals with roles within a project team, as does Assignment 4.4. Here too, fellow students will discuss your role and you will consider the roles of your fellow students. Your fellow students will also complete this assignment. However, the starting point now is not a test (as it was in the previous section) but a number of characterisations. We have learned from experience that characterisations are a good tool for determining who plays which roles within the team, and the strengths and weaknesses related to those roles.

Assignment 4.5 Which group role?

This assignment is an adaptation of an assignment by Van Ruymbeke et al (1987) and concerns group roles. Every member of the project group will complete the group role chart of this assignment.

a   *Completing the group role chart*
·   Take the chart in Appendix 5, Group roles.
·   Fill in all the names of your fellow students at the top of the group role list (including your own name).
·   For each fellow student – and yourself – tick which roles are filled in the group. Note: you do not have to tick the same number of roles for all students.

b   *Discussing the charts*
In a meeting (if necessary, chaired by the tutor), place the charts next to one another. Each individual group member should be mentioned during this discussion. Check whether there are many differences between the completed charts or not.

As a group, do the following:
·   For each group member check which roles have been mentioned most, and which arguments have been given for it.
·   Let the group indicate which strong and weaker points this member possesses, and also how they relate to those roles.
·   Let the group member himself indicate if he agrees with the roles assigned to him and why.
·   Let the group member also indicate which weaker points he wants to change if any, and how he plans to do that.

Record all this in written minutes immediately. After completing this (and after you have established which roles belong to which members), have a brief group evaluation. The main questions to ask are:

- Which roles occur most often in the group?
- Which strengths and weaknesses occur most?
- How does the group function?
    - What went well?
    - What did not go well?
    - Which roles were lacking in the group and what effect did this have?
    - What is the overall assessment?

c Subsequent reflection

Next, make an individual report on this assignment. In it, deal with:
- The roles assigned to you by the group (and why)
- The related strengths and weaknesses assigned to you by the group (and why)
- The roles assigned to you by yourself and the strengths and weaknesses you recognize

Finish with a brief conclusion: how do you think you function, what might you like to change, and why?

 Enter the reports of part *a, b* and *c* of this assignment in your PDP Toolbox in the Assignments section. Also update your Personality Profile concerning the weak and strong points you have according to the Belbin roles.

Enter the study targets and improvement points you have found in *c* as action points in the PDP Action Points and logbook section of the PDP Toolbox.

4.6 Four communication styles

The Dutch communication specialist Frank Oomkes (1998) distinguishes four styles of communication and four related types of people: the action type, the tactical type, the human type and the ideas type. According to Oomkes, each individual is a combination of these types. No one has all the traits of any one style, if only because no one has just the one style. The styles, of course, are related to strengths and weaknesses: action-type people have different strengths and weaknesses from those of ideas-type people. In brief: once you know which styles suit you most, you will also have an insight into questions such as 'Who am I?' and 'What can I do?' The styles also provide information about the question 'Where do I fit in?' An action-type person cannot function very well in an ideas-type team, whilst he positively blossoms in an action-type team. However, this information is only a tool – it is not intended to compartmentalise people, which is equally true of the Belbin test or of completing Enneagrams such as those in Chapter 2.

We shall now provide a brief sketch of each of these communication styles:

Action types

Action types like to be busy, to perform well, to gain practical results, to solve problems, to improve situations in a practical way. They are particularly focused on results, practical targets, productivity, challenges, efficiency, changes and decisions. They are often very practical, quick to make decisions, very 'direct', impatient. They are energetic and go straight for what they want. They like people who can explain precisely the practical use of their ideas. Action types fit well into the technical sectors of product organisations.

Tactical types

Tactical types like to apply structure, to organise, to outline strategies (setting long-term targets), to devise tactics (i.e. think up what needs to be done and in which sequence to attain strategic goals). They are focused particularly on planning and organisation, on process control, and on analysing and testing the processes. They are systematic, logical, patient, focused on solid and verifiable facts, and they are careful and not emotional. They like people who present facts exactly, point by point, in a logical way. They fit well into management functions, political and higher management.

Human types

Human types like everything that motivates people, i.e. social processes, communication and team work. They are focused in particular on good cooperation, good working relations, feelings, understanding the other people's standards and values. They are attentive, sensitive, sympathetic, understanding and observant, warm, spontaneous and emotional. They are more subjective than objective, more emotional than rational. They like people who approach them informally, who do not get down to business immediately (who like to chat first), and when you put a proposal to them, the first thing they want to know is which people support that proposal. They often function well as managers, leaders, advisors and therapeutic workers.

Ideas types

Ideas types love to exchange ideas, innovation and creativity, and they like to work with theories and theoretical concepts. They also like deduction (explaining facts and phenomena from general laws) and induction (deducing laws from various facts and phenomena). They are focused particularly on new chances and new methods, on master plans and discovering internal relations no one has noticed before, on explanations and completely new ways of solving problems. They are creative, full of ideas, challenging, charismatic (their ideas are very appealing), but sometimes self-willed, difficult to follow and unrealistic. They often get sidetracked. They like people who are willing to spend time on forming ideas, and they like to be presented with unique ideas that are related to theoretical concepts. They often function well as scientists, inventors and artists.

Assignment 4.6 Which style of communication?

This assignment may be used purely for self-reflection, in which case, complete part *a* only. However, it may also be used for self-reflection and group assessment. In that case, complete parts *b* and *c* as well.

a Personal evaluation

Appendix 6 is a questionnaire with which you can determine your communication styles according to Oomkes.

- Complete the test by circling your choices.
- On the basis of the score list determine which communication styles from the Oomkes test fit you best.
- Indicate which styles you think fit you best, and why. In other words, is the test result correct? Give examples of why you think certain styles fit you best.
- Write down your strongest points (at least two), and indicate how they match this mix of styles. Support your answer with examples.
- Write down your weakest points (at least two). Indicate how they match the mix of styles mentioned previously. Also indicate whether this represents an 'allergy' or 'pitfall' (see Section 2.4). Example: 'results-focused' is a quality belonging to the action type, an 'allergy' of it can be 'too focused on results' or 'impatient', and impatience is indeed a characteristic of being action-orientated.

b Group assessment

- Indicate for each student of your theme group which style(s) you recognise in him/her, and state briefly why.
- Indicate (with a brief explanation) which related strengths and weaknesses you recognise in each student.
- Indicate the dominant style (or mix of styles) of the group as a whole. Please provide a brief explanation with examples.
- Indicate whether the group functions well. That is, indicate the strongest point, the weakest point and an overall assessment. Also indicate whether the functioning is related to that style: for example, 'the group is too action-focused and consequently functions poorly. This is apparent from....', or, 'The group functions well because it is both action and idea-focused. This is apparent from...'.
- Indicate how you 'fit in' with the group (given its style).

c Subsequent discussion

Discuss these findings with the group, with or without the tutor as chairperson. Make sure to do the following:

- First list the opinions about the group as a whole: what do the group members think of the style (or mix of styles) of the group as a whole, and how well does the group function?
- Then check each individual student.
- List the styles his fellow students think he has and check whether they match his own.
- Give feedback on his strong and weaker points.

Record all this in the minutes and, if the tutor wishes, also in an individual self-reflection report. The latter should deal with:

- Your styles and the related strengths and weaknesses (see Part 1);
- The feedback on it provided by your fellow students and tutor.

 Enter the reports of parts *a*, *b* and *c* of this assignment in your PDP Toolbox in the Assignments section. Update your Personality Profile and enter the study targets and points for improvement you have found in the PDP Action Points section and logbook of the PDP Toolbox.

4.7   Behaviour in a team

A team may consist of many different kinds of people. While the Belbin test (see Section 4.3) provides information on various team roles, so do the four behaviour types of the MDI (see Section 3.3). Bonnstetter et al (1993) state that each type wants to be approached in a different manner. Sometimes it is good to know which type you are dealing with as this may prevent inappropriate ways of approaching people.

So how do you communicate with a 'red', 'yellow', 'green' or 'blue' type?

Communicating with a 'red' type: be clear, concise and 'to the point'. Stay businesslike and do not engage in 'chit-chat'. Do not be evasive and do not take his assertiveness as an attack. Stand up for yourself. Never confront him with a set decision: always leave room for options and alternatives. Be clear about the goals, and present your case in a logical and efficient manner. In the event of disagreement, concentrate on the facts.

Communicating with a 'yellow' type: take time for the social aspect (never be short), give him space to express his dreams and opinions, entertain him with stories and anecdotes, listen to his imaginative stories and anecdotes, let him do things in his own time, stimulate him with ideas and jokes but do keep things going, do not lay down the law to him, ask his opinion and do not be impersonal or purely focused on the task.

Communicating with a 'green' type: start with some personal remarks to break the ice (i.e. do not start with business right away), show interest in him as a person, patiently enquire about his personal ideas and goals, approach him tactfully (he does not like surprises), allow him time to finish thinking and to reach a decision (do not rush him), when disagreeing support your opinion with facts and with arguments from people the green type respects, do not take compliance too quickly as indicating satisfaction (sometimes green types say 'yes', but act 'no'), be nice to him and express your appreciation, be informal but straightforward and make sure your behaviour is non-threatening.

Communicating with a 'blue' type: be well prepared, approach him with consideration, look at all sides of the matter together, set up a plan of action (with targets and a time schedule) containing exactly what needs to happen, pay close attention to details and make good your promises, when disagreeing support your opinion with exact facts or the opinions of a respected authority (never try playing on his feelings), provide him with plenty of information and the time needed to make decisions, and make sure (in particular) that you give him private time to analyse his thoughts.

Assignment 4.7 Which behaviour?

a Preparation
- Read carefully through the theory about different types ('behaviour colours') in Section 3.4.
- Which type fits you best? Provide a brief explanation.
- Indicate two strengths and weaknesses you think are related to your behavioural type.
- Indicate to what extent this group (with this assignment) is also your 'ideal work environment'. Consult the theory in Section 3.4.
- Indicate whether the tips given for good communication with your type hold true for you as well. Note: if, as you see it, you score high on these two types, you should check the tips for both types!
- Indicate to what extent the other students actually approach you in the manner you like.
- Indicate for each student in your team which type (or combination of types) you recognise in him/her. Provide arguments and examples.
- For each student give two strengths and two weaknesses relating to the type he/she is according to you. Explain your answer briefly.
- Indicate what you think is the prevailing type in the group and whether that strengthens the group or not.

b Subsequent discussion with the group as a whole
Organise a discussion with the group, with or without the teacher or tutor as chairman. Take minutes of this meeting. As a group, do the following:
- For each student, determine which behavioural type he recognises in himself and which type the others see in him.
- For each student, provide feedback on strengths and weaknesses relating to his behavioural type.
- Let each student respond to the question of:
    - Whether the communication tips match his specific case
    - Whether this group (with this assignment) is a good work environment for him
    - Whether he is approached in the right way by his fellow group members
- Finally, determine the most prevalent types in the group, and whether they strengthen the group or not.

c Individual reflection report
- What do you think is your most characteristic behaviour, and what are the related strengths and weaknesses?
- What do your fellow students think is your most characteristic behaviour and its related strengths and weaknesses?
- In this discussion you will also have become aware of your fellow students' predominant types. Which of the related communication tips will you use and which not? Why?

 Make a report of this assignment in your PDP Toolbox in the Assignments section.

4.8   Team-building and team roles

To make a team function better (a team that is already good can still be improved), team-building is important. This can be achieved in various ways: building rafts in the Ardennes, a pub crawl with all your friends, eating out together and so on. But you can also reinforce a team by group assessments focusing on the performance of individuals and the team as a whole. This book contains various assignments of that kind. The following assignment is intended to assess whether all task and atmosphere roles are adequately represented in your team. You can combine this assignment with Assignment 4.3, in which the same applies, based on Belbin's team roles theory, or with the group assessment in Section 4.2.

The division within this section is based on Reijnders (1997).

Team roles can be divided into three groups:
1   Task roles
2   Atmosphere roles
3   Dysfunctional roles

Re 1   Task roles
- The initiator: takes the initiative, makes activities start
- Structurer: applies structure, makes connections, summarises various opinions and keeps a tight grip on things
- Implementer: checks that everything that is thought of is implemented, makes practical work schedules, organises activities, handles things that are otherwise forgotten
- Explorer: constantly brings up new ideas or unexpected solutions to problems, looks beyond the tried and tested
- Investigator: digs deeper into things, gathers information, prepares the theory well

Re 2   Atmosphere roles
- Humorist: makes jokes and improves the atmosphere
- Relativist: puts problems in perspective, stays calm in times of stress, looks at things from a different angle, differentiates things to make them look better
- Mediator: searches for compromises, mediates in conflicts
- Listener: listens to everybody, shows appreciation, can empathise with others
- Optimist: always sees things as positive and always sees a way out

Re 3   Dysfunctional roles
- Aggressor: is very critical and domineering and nags too much
- Passive person: does not contribute enough, is often uninterested
- Cynic: quickly loses faith, quickly gives up because 'it won't work anyway', is very critical about many things
- Negative person: takes a negative view of everything

A harmonious team will not have too many people who often play dysfunctional roles. 'Dysfunctional' is not necessarily always bad – sometimes there has to be an aggressor, for example, for a little while, but too much can be harmful. Furthermore, it is useful that the atmosphere and task roles are on the whole filled. A team in which its members play task roles exclusively will be very dull. A team in which its members play atmosphere roles exclusively will make no progress at all unless someone takes on a task role. In fact, a team top-heavy in any one role will fail to be effective either – think of the mess that is likely to result when you put four 'initiative takers' together without one 'structurer'. Or think of a group of eight 'explorers' without an 'implementer' – rich in ideas but leading to nothing.

Synergy

In a combination of roles there is synergy: the roles reinforce each other. The explorer has ideas that the implementer has not; the implementer is better in practical realisation. They reinforce each other. This is why it is good to have both roles in a team, or in one person. Of course, it is wonderful when someone is both an implementer and explorer.

For the assessment of the team and your functioning in it, it is useful to find out how the roles are divided among the team members and which roles you fill. That is the assignment. Remember that no one has only one role. Investigate in particular which combination of roles fits you. Also investigate whether those roles show synergy.

Assignment 4.8 Which team roles?

a Preparation
- Which task roles, atmosphere roles and dysfunctional roles do you fill in the team? And do you fill them in the right way? Is there synergy between those roles? Explain and give examples.
- Also state your strongest and weaker points in relation to this. Provide a brief explanation and examples.
- Then, on the basis of the two previous questions, indicate whether you function well within this team or not.
- For each student indicate which task roles, atmosphere roles and dysfunctional roles he fills within the team. Also discuss his related strengths and weaknesses briefly. For each fellow student provide a brief explanation of your answer.
- State your opinion about the group as a whole. Which roles are represented best and which roles the worst? Is there synergy between the various roles? What is your overall judgement of the group?

b Subsequent discussion
Discuss these findings with the whole group, with or without the tutor as chairman. Take minutes of the meeting. As a group, do the following:
- Determine for each student which roles he has according to his fellow students. Also discuss his strengths and weaknesses. As a group, assess his functioning.
- Then determine which roles occur in the team as a whole. Which are well represented? Which are over-represented? How is there synergy? Which roles are lacking?

- State your opinion about the group as a whole. What goes well? What needs improving? How?

c *Individual reflection report*
- Which roles did you assign yourself, and which strengths and weaknesses?
- Which roles did the group assign to you, and which strengths and weaknesses?
- What is now your overall assessment of yourself (and your strengths and weaknesses)?
- Indicate what you plan to do in any following project. Which strengths will you exploit there, and which weaknesses will you want to improve? How?

 Enter the reports of parts *a, b* and *c* of this assignment in your PDP Toolbox in the Assignments section. Update your Personality Profile and enter the study targets and points of improvement you have found in the PDP Action Points section and logbook of the PDP Toolbox.

4.9   Updating the PDP

After completing all (or at least most) of the preceding assignments, you will have given many answers to the question 'What can I do in a team?' Group assessments aided by the Belbin test yield different information from other types of group assessment. It is useful to compare the various results and so arrive at a complete picture.

At the end of Chapter 2 you made a PDP in the Toolbox based on assignments concerning the question 'Who am I?'. At the end of Chapter 3 you updated the PDP, paying particular attention to your skills as an individual. Now update your PDP again, this time concentrating on your skills as a team worker.

Assignment 4.9 Updating your PDP
 Begin by reading through all the reports you made of the assignments in this chapter. Proceed to the Personality Profile section of the PDP Toolbox and fill in everything you can on the basis of the completed assignments.

What do I want to become?

5

5.1 Your future sphere of employment
5.2 Analysing situations vacant
5.3 Visiting a company
5.4 Sphere of employment research
5.5 Research into employment possibilities
5.6 My dream job

'Made to be a nurse!' 'He was born to be a teacher!' or 'He will follow in his father's footsteps!' Did you hear this type of remark when you were a child? Possibly so often that you now think: 'Me a nurse? Never! Do the same as my father? Forget it!' But what *do* you want to do?

To find out which profession suits you, you will have to investigate your future sphere of employment. It is never too early to start working on this during your studies. The labour market is vast and extremely varied and sometimes you may have an incorrect perception of the profession that appeals to you most at a given moment. By familiarising yourself with the labour market as soon as possible, and actively looking for information, you will discover what the labour market has to offer and which function suits you best. Furthermore, if you have a clear idea of what you want, you will be in a better position to choose your individual study areas.

In the previous chapters you will have gained an insight into who you are and which competencies you already have or must develop. This chapter contains assignments that will help you find the information necessary for choosing a profession that you want and will be able to have.

After familiarising yourself with your future sphere of employment through professional organisations, you will analyse suitable situations vacant. Next, you will prepare for a visit to a company and later make the visit. You will interview a professional person, after which you will give a presentation about the interview.

5.1 Your future sphere of employment

Sphere of employment

On the day they hand you your diploma, will you know what that piece of paper enables you to do? It is important to familiarise yourself with the labour market during your studies thereby after your studies avoiding going to work for a company that does not really suit you, or ending up in a position you do not want. First of all, you must investigate your future sphere of employment. In choosing your studies you have already chosen a direction for your future and for a specific sector or sphere of employment. Assignment 5.1 is about doing a detailed investigation of your future sphere of employment.

Being aware of your sphere of employment can also stimulate you in your studies: you will know what you are doing things for, and that can mean just that extra little push to complete that difficult module.

Professional organisation

Most professions fall under a particular sector – the agricultural or the health care sector, for instance – and have their own professional trade organisations which can provide a wealth of information on the sphere of employment they represent. In addition to providing general information on professions they can also supply information about specific professions and related competencies. Not only can they supply information on various fields of employment and ongoing developments, but also on the expectations of the sector for the future, labour conditions, salary scales, and so on.

Tip: some trade organisations publish a branch-related magazine – usually free for students – that keeps you abreast of the developments in that particular sphere of employment.

Assignment 5.1 Employment image

You enrolled for your studies because you have a specific perception of the profession you would like to be working in later. For example, you chose architecture because you know someone who loves working in the construction area. Or you have opted for information science because you like the idea of 'doing something with computers'. It is important to indicate why you chose this particular type of training. What are you passionate about? In the following assignments you will investigate whether your expectations match reality.
- What is the name of the job you hope to be doing later?
- What will your daily tasks consist of?
- Where will you be working? Inside, outside; city, in the country?
- What is the office likely to look like?
- Will you have much contact with colleagues or clients?
- What do you want to attain in your job?
- Do you want to make a steady career?
- Do you want to make a lot of money?
- Enumerate five characteristics which make this profession attractive to you.

Discuss the results with your teacher/tutor or with your group.

Assignment 5.2 Required competencies

a Make a list of things you want to know about your future sphere of employment.

b Start looking for the professional or trade organisation best suited to your specialisation or training. These organisations are easily traced through the Internet, but you can also ask your teacher. Contact the right professional organisation and ask for information about possible jobs.

c Make a comprehensive list of competencies needed for the jobs under b.

 For each competency under c provide a description in your PDP Toolbox in the Competencies and Competency profile section. Do this according to the guidelines in Assignment 1.2. For each competency indicate what information, skills and attitude are needed.

Assignment 5.3 Competencies still to be attained

When you completed the assignments in Chapters 3 and 4 you entered in your PDP Toolbox those competencies you have already attained. Now compare the competencies you should have, according to your professional organisation, with the competencies you have already attained.

a Indicate to what extent you have attained certain competencies.

c Which competencies will you be working on next?

d How will you do that?

e When will you know whether you have mastered this competency?

 Enter answer a in your PDP Toolbox in the Competencies and Competency profile section. Indicate to what extent you have attained certain competencies – you can do this by indicating a percentage. When you have mastered the competency in full you should write down 100%, plus the date on which you feel you mastered it. This rounds off the competency.

Enter the points for improvement found under c, d and e as action points under the PDP Action Points section and in the logbook of the PDP Toolbox.

5.2 Analysing situations vacant

Situations vacant

Companies looking for new employees advertise for them in various ways. Traditionally, these job offers appear as situations vacant in trade magazines and newspapers. Nowadays, job offers are increasingly appearing on the Internet as well. Some people read the situations vacant pages in newspapers and magazines carefully, while others merely skim them. Many students start reading job offers only at the end of their studies – when they are actually looking for a job. Yet it is preferable to start reading job offers carefully to check which jobs are available long before you start looking for a job. First of all, doing so will provide you with information about possible jobs by making you aware of various functions, approximately what these functions entail, and which competency demands are being made. Secondly, you will find out which jobs appeal to you most. If you already had a certain position in mind, this will represent a confirmation of your plans. If there is a disparity between the job description and what you had in mind, you may have to modify your personal development plan, and hence your study plan. Thirdly, you will know ahead of time what prospects there are in your direction and how many jobs are available in your field.

Finally, familiarising yourself early on with the labour market may motivate you to finish your studies as quickly as possible. Alternatively, it may motivate you to make your studies more coherent – after all, you will have a clearer picture of where you want to go – by adapting your internships and choice of studies to the desired job.

Assignment 5.4 Jobs on offer research

For the period of a month, gather all jobs on offer from newspapers, magazines and the Internet that appeal to you. Based on the following list of questions, evaluate your personal job folder:

a How many jobs are there on average in the newspaper for you? Is that encouraging or disappointing?
b Which jobs appeal to you? Why?
c In which field were the jobs on offer?
d What are the requirements for your desired jobs?
e How do you measure up to these requirements? What do you need to work on?
f If you met the requirements for the various jobs, which would you apply for and which not?

Make a report of this assignment in your PDP Toolbox in the Assignments section.

Assignment 5.5 The labour market

a For a period of one month, gather as many articles as possible from newspapers and magazines relating to the labour market in your field specifically.
b On the basis of the articles gathered, describe the future prospects of the sector you are being trained for.

Make a report of this assignment in your PDP Toolbox in the Assignments section.

Assignment 5.6 Companies in your professional field

Investigate two relatively different companies/organisations operating in your professional field. Gather information on the companies, through for example:

· the Internet
· the Chamber of Commerce
· the company itself, by means of annual reports, brochures, etc.

Make a report of this assignment in your PDP Toolbox in the Assignments section.

5.3   Visiting a company

After doing the job on offer analysis of Section 5.2 you will have an idea of a company or organisation which you would like to work for and are qualified to work for.

This section is about preparing for, making and evaluating a visit or excursion to a company. Afterwards, you will write a report on the visit. The goal of the visit is to get to know a company operating in your professional field and to speak with employees of that company who have the job which you are being trained for or in which you are interested.

The idea is to organise the visit together with some fellow students. It is important you do this in consultation with your tutor or teacher. After all, your school tries to have a good relationship with the companies close by, and a poorly organised excursion could seriously damage such a relationship!

The following subjects may appear in your report:
·   The company set-up (what is the company ethos, what departments does it have, who is responsible to whom, how many branches are there, etc).
·   The company in numbers (number of employees, number of products, profits, etc).
·   The company's target. The target is the goal set up by the company itself, usually formulated in a concise, catchy phrase.
·   The company's aims: what does the company want to achieve?
·   The company's products or services.
·   The primary process: what processes are involved in delivering the main product or service?
·   The company culture: do staff members work well together? What are the rules (both written and unwritten)? What taboos are there?
·   New developments within the company (new products, new techniques, etc).
·   Processes related to your professional field in the company.
·   A job description of one or more employees working in your professional field in the company. What kind of tasks are done?

Would you like to work for this company? Why/why not?
What position would you like to have in this company? Does this position match the results of Assignment 5.1, Employment image?

Make sure to discuss with your teacher which points on this list you will work on in your report.

Assignment 5.7 Preparing to go on an excursion
a   Together with your teacher assemble a group to organise the visit.
b   Find a suitable company in terms of your training.
c   Investigate the company (over the Internet) and make an extended list of questions you would like to have answered. Consult the list of topics for this.
d   If necessary, review the list of questions with your teacher.

e Enter the questions you have prepared in your PDP Toolbox in the Assignments section.

f Make a step-by-step plan for the visit. Ask your teacher for his approval.

g Approach the company together with your teacher. Make sure to get a good overall picture of the company, try to arrange a tour and talk to one or more employees doing a job that is of interest to your group.

h Bring along a thank-you for the tour guides.

Enter the excursion plan in your PDP Toolbox in the Assignments section.

Assignment 5.8 The excursion

Take pen and paper on your visit and make plenty of notes about any presentations, talks and the tour. Use these notes for your report. Gather as much other material as possible to use for your report.

Assignment 5.9 Evaluating the excursion

a Use the data from Assignments 5.6 and 5.7 as the basis for a structured report on the excursion.

b Would you want to work for this company? Why/why not?

c State three positive aspects and three negative aspects of the work performed by the employees operating in your professional field in the company.

Enter this report in your PDP Toolbox in the Assignments section.

5.4 Sphere of employment research

You will have noticed the importance of the questions 'What do I want?' and 'Where do I fit in?' in the PDP. This is why it is important to have an idea of possible employment after your studies and why it is useful to interview someone who performs work you could be doing in the future. He can tell you exactly what is attractive and less attractive about his job, what the challenges are, what his working day looks like and so on. He will also be able to tell you what knowledge and which skills you will need later.

Since you are enquiring about what you find important, there is no standard list of questions. Here are some suggestions:
- You could ask the person about the link between his/her studies and the job. Did his/her study connect well with the job? Which courses were especially useful and why? Did the person interviewed need additional or different training? What kind of courses were they and what did they teach him?
- Did the person interviewed learn much from his internship? What exactly? Did he/she find that doing an internship opened doors to a permanent job? If so, in what way?
- How did the person interviewed get his job? Did the people who hired him only take into consideration his studies, or did other issues play a role? Which skills were taken into consideration?

- What are the future plans of the person interviewed? Does he/she want to advance? Does the job offer growth possibilities?
- How satisfied with his/her job does the person interviewed seem, and how satisfied would you be with it? Think of income, time spent, degree of variety, how interesting the various tasks are, and so on.
- What are the specific tasks of the person interviewed? Do they appeal to you or not? Which skills does he/she need for his job? And what level of knowledge?

Bear in mind that these are only suggestions. The main thing is that the interview will hopefully help you to answer more satisfactorily the questions 'What do I want to do?' and 'Where do I fit in?'.

Assignment 5.10 Conducting an interview with a professional
Adopt the following procedure for the interview (and discuss the procedure with your teacher).
a Read Section 6.6, The interview in preparation.
b Determine the goal of the interview as precisely as possible. Which profession do you want to know more about, why and what exactly? Try as much as possible to address the important issues.

Do you want a job with a lot of responsibility? Ask the person interviewed about the responsibilities of his job, and ask how extensive those responsibilities are. Do you find it important to have time for hobbies and relaxation aside from the job? Ask the person interviewed how demanding his job is. Do you just want to know how a manager works in practice? Ask pointed questions on that subject. You can only start writing down the questions when you know your goal.
c Find a suitable candidate. Do not look for candidates in your family circle or circle of friends – you are unlikely to learn anything new from them! Once you have found a candidate, phone him/her or write him/her a letter. Inform him/her briefly about the goal of the interview and make an appointment.
d Prepare a list of well-considered questions.
e Do the interview.

 Write a report on the basis of the interview and enter it in your PDP Toolbox in the Assignments section.

Assignment 5.11 Presenting the interview
Assignment 5.9 involved interviewing a professional in your professional field. Consult with your teacher whether you should do this current assignment or not, because it does require considerable organisation.
a Prepare a brief presentation based on the interview you had.
b Present the results. Make sure your presentation is as inclusive as possible.
c After the presentation, have a discussion about which competencies the professional needs.

Write a report based on your report and enter it in your PDP Toolbox in the Assignments section.

5.5 Research into employment possibilities

One day, you will have received your diploma and will start looking for a job. You will apply for each and every job vacancy you think is suitable for you. Based on your letter of application you are invited for an interview and you get the job! You start out with the best intentions, but after a while you find you are not enjoying your work. You discover that you have made the wrong choice. Not only is this bad for you, but also for your employer. He will lose a good employee, and you will have to start looking for another job.

Demands

By carefully monitoring in advance which demands and wishes you have for a job, you will avoid as far as possible going to work for the wrong company. While there is no avoiding the demands of a job, you would no doubt like to have the job meet your expectations.

The following three assignments will help you investigate which factors are generally important when making career choices. We are not concerned here with what you consider important factors – that will come later.

Assignment 5.12 Investigating work locations

Whether someone wakes up cheerful in the morning and enjoys going to work depends on a large number of factors relating to both his position and his private life. The location where someone works has an influence on his job enjoyment.

He may have a challenging and fascinating job abroad, but may also be homesick for his relatives and home town. If so, he is probably not in the right position.

Table 5.1 **Advantages and disadvantages of particular work locations**

Work location	Disadvantage	Advantage
In a city	1 2 3	1 2 3
In the country	1 2 3	1 2 3
In the national region	1 2 3	1 2 3
Abroad	1 2 3	1 2 3

Table 5.1 lists work locations. For each location, give three reasons why these may have a positive influence and three reasons why these may have a negative influence on the work environment. For example, living and working in the country has the advantage of not having to sit in a traffic jam in the morning. However, a disadvantage is that you have to travel a distance if you want to attend a concert at night.

Fill in Table 5.1 as fully as possible. Use the information you have gathered by doing the other assignments in this chapter, ask others in your environment or have a group discussion with fellow students.

 Write a report of this assignment in your PDP Toolbox in the Assignments section.

Assignment 5.13 Investigating organisational characteristics

Whether someone feels comfortable in an organisation (company/institution, etc) or not can depend on, for example, the size of the organisation. One person can feel completely at home in a small company because he can perform many different tasks, while another will choose a large organisation because he is able to specialise or has more chances of promotion.

Table 5.2 **Organisational characteristics**

Organisation characteristic	Is appealing because	Is less appealing because
Working in a small organisation (< 25 employees)	1 2 3	1 2 3
Working in a medium size organisation (25 – 100 employees)	1 2 3	1 2 3
Working in a large organisation (> 100 employees)	1 2 3	1 2 3
Working in a commercial organisation (profit)	1 2 3	1 2 3
Working in a non-commercial organisation (non-profit)	1 2 3	1 2 3
Working in an organisation with a project-based approach	1 2 3	1 2 3

	Is important because	Is not important because
Agreeable company atmosphere	1 2 3	1 2 3
Stimulating management	1 2 3	1 2 3
Appealing products and services	1 2 3	1 2 3

a Fill in Table 5.2 as completely as possible. Use the information you have gathered with the other assignments in this chapter, ask others in your environment, or have a group discussion with fellow students.

b If necessary, add points you find important to the chart.

 Write a report of this assignment in your PDP Toolbox in the Assignments section.

Table 5.3 **Job characteristics**

Job characteristics	Is not important because	Is important because
Independence	1 2 3	1 2 3
Challenging position	1 2 3	1 2 3
Varied work	1 2 3	1 2 3
Growth possibilities	1 2 3	1 2 3
Work under stress/time pressure	1 2 3	1 2 3
Team work	1 2 3	1 2 3
Good salary	1 2 3	1 2 3
Good secondary labour conditions	1 2 3	1 2 3
Financial security	1 2 3	1 2 3
Training possibilities	1 2 3	1 2 3
Working hours	1 2 3	1 2 3
Travel	1 2 3	1 2 3
Commitment, social involvement	1 2 3	1 2 3

Assignment 5.14 Investigating job characteristics

One person wants to make a lot of money and is prepared to work hard for it, another finds leisure time more important. He does not want to spend too much time on his job and settles for lower wages. If you are not too concerned about money, it is worthwhile investigating why someone else is concerned about it. Maybe you will discover it is not such a bad idea to make a lot of money now, so that you can stop work when you are 50. Or you may find out that a challenging position is so demanding that at night you can only flop down on the sofa, completely exhausted. Everyone has their own special demands and wishes concerning a job. Table 5.3 shows you a list of possible personal wishes and demands. Indicate for each wish or demand whether it is important to you or not.

a Fill in Table 5.3 as completely as possible. Use the information you have gathered in the other assignments in this chapter. Ask others in your environment or have a discussion with your group.
b If possible, add points you find important to the chart.

 Write a report of this assignment in your PDP Toolbox in the Assignments section.

....

5.6 My dream job

Dream job

By the final stages of your study you will have started looking for a job. You are not just looking for any position but one that fits you perfectly. And you want to have a job with a good employer. In brief, you start looking for your dream job. Maybe you will not find it immediately, but the motto is: 'He who does not know where he wants to go will never get there!'

In the next two assignments – representing a combination of the three previous ones – you will describe your dream job. In doing this, you should make a distinction between demands and wishes. The demands you make of your job are the minimum conditions under which you want to work. Make sure your demands are realistic. An executive position with a multinational is unattainable for a beginner in the labour market. However, it may be your wish to be an executive manager sometime in the future.

....

Assignment 5.15 Minimum job requirements

In Assignments 5.11 to 5.13 you investigated job requirements. Read through them before answering the following questions. You will now formulate your own requirements for a job:
· In which sector or sectors do you want to work? In which do you definitely not want to work?
· What are your financial demands?
· In which location do you want to work? See Assignment 5.11.
· What characteristics should the company you want to work for have? See Assignment 5.12.
· What are your job/position requirements? See Assignment 5.13.

Write a report of this assignment in your PDP Toolbox in the Assignments section.

Assignment 5.16 Your dream job

In the previous assignment you determined the minimum demands your job must meet. You decided which position you aspire to, how much money you want to make, whether you want to work abroad or in your own area, and so on. But you also have wishes: you may aspire to work in a certain sector eventually, or in a management position. This is your ultimate dream job.

Answer the following questions as specifically as possible. Use the results of Assignments 5.11 to 5.14. For each answer provide three reasons why you have these wishes.
·   Which position would you eventually like to work in?
·   How much money would you eventually like to earn?
·   Where would you eventually like to work?
·   What other wishes do you have?

 Write a report of this assignment in your PDP Toolbox in the Assignments section.

Finding a fascinating job is sometimes a matter of luck, but you may give that luck a little help. By doing the assignments in this chapter you have been actively engaged in familiarising yourself with the labour market. You have discovered there are many possibilities open to you, and now you know in which direction you should start looking for a job. You have gained an insight into the demands you make of a job and what your wishes are. Not all your wishes will be fulfilled in your first job. Not being eligible for a certain position is, among other things, related to your level of competency. By looking ahead, you can make a careful analysis of the competencies you must have to be able to work in the job you aspire to.

Assignment 5.17 Step-by-step plan for getting your dream job

Proceed as follows:
a   Describe the competencies you need for your dream job and indicate the level at which you should have these competencies.
b   In your PDP you will find a description of your current competencies and related levels. Put these two lists next to each other and record the differences. You now have a description of the competencies you still have to develop.
c   Determine your goals and set up a step-by-step plan.

 Write a report of this assignment in your PDP Toolbox in the Assignments section.

Tip: Remember, each choice you make is not necessarily a choice for life. You can always adjust your plans. Do not be afraid to make the wrong choices.

Assignment 5.18 Applying for a job

a Consult the weekend edition of one or more national or regional newspaper. You can also use a trade magazine that shows job offers in your professional field.

- Choose a position that fits you (if possible, your dream job).
- Investigate the relationship between that job and your competencies. Do this as follows:
  - Enumerate the main job demands.
  - Indicate which strengths from your personality profile and professional competency profile match these demands. You can find your personality profile and competency profile in your PDP Toolbox in the Personal Profile and Competencies sections. Also check Sections 3.12 and 3.13.

b Apply for the job.
- Write your letter of application. Give convincing reasons and your motivation for meeting the job demands. In Section 6.8 you will find useful tips for this.
- Write a curriculum vitae. Use the information from Section 6.9 and your personality profile in the Toolbox.
- Should you be invited to an interview, use the tips in Section 6.10.

Tools

This chapter describes tools and techniques that have already been used in the previous chapters of this book. You will also find topics that expand the contents of previous chapters slightly.

Throughout the course of your studies you must think on a regular basis of your own study targets, formulate them and reformulate them. The first section deals with a systematical method that you can use as an aid and this can be supplemented by a logbook.

During your studies you will give feedback to others and receive feedback from others. For the latter, active listening is important. We explain this in three subsequent sections.

To gather information from others you may use an interview. In Section 6.6 you will find tips on interviewing.

To use your time better (i.e. more efficiently and effectively) time management is important. If you follow the recommendations in Section 6.7 you will lose less time.

The chapter concludes with three sections containing instructions which will prove useful in applying for a job.

6.1 Study targets in four steps

The setting of study targets in steps is treated specifically in Assignments 3.2, 3.8, 3.9 and 3.13.

An investigation of companies and educational institutions has provided a clear conclusion: study targets are useful, but they must be specific, measurable, motivating and attainable. This is, of course, logical. After all, you should not have vague study targets, and what good are study targets that do not motivate you?

Four-step method

Therefore, set up your study targets according to the following four-step method:

Four-step method

Step 1 Being specific
Describe in detail *what* you want and *why*. You can do that by answering the following questions (the so-called '6 w's'):
- What exactly do you intend to do?
- When?
- Where?
- Why (directed towards the past: *which* problem you want to solve, *what* you want to change and for what *reason* you want that, etc)?
- What purpose (directed towards the future: what do you want to achieve and why)?
- How?

'To be happy' is not specific enough. 'Climbing the company ladder' is more specific, but still not specific enough. So if you want to be promoted, fill in all the w's stating exactly which position you want, in what department in the company, and at what salary. Under 'for what purpose' indicate exactly the advantages you expect from this promotion, and so on. You must answer the question 'for what purpose' exactly: you must know your goal: i.e., have a clear idea of what you are striving for. The question about 'why' is important too: that is the question about your motivation. For example: 'In each project group meeting I will put forward my views and give good reasons for holding them, and I will do so on three occasions' may answer the question of what you intend to do, but not why you are going to do it! You may be choosing this study target because you think your wonderful ideas are not getting sufficient exposure, but also because you are afraid to open your mouth and want to do something about that.

Step 2 Subdividing (plan of action)
After specifying your goal, you must identify sub-goals. To do that, indicate which part-time activities (or intermediary steps) are necessary to reach your goal. Suppose you specified 'getting a promotion' in Step 1, then your sub-goals could be:
- To have talks in various departments in order to gauge the possibilities
- To take on more tasks in your current position that are integral to the position you desire

- To complete courses or training exercises that make you more suitable for the position desired

Sub-goals allow you to measure whether you are going in the right direction – did I attain my sub-goals at the planned moment or not? So set up a plan of action by indicating as precisely as possible what you intend to do and in what sequence to reach your goal.

Step 3 Making it measurable
After having specified the goal and divided it into subsections, make it measurable. Here are some examples:
- By 20 November at the latest I will make an appointment with the head of Human Resources for a talk on promotion possibilities within the company.
- By 20 October at the latest I must have made at least 12 phone calls to people who should be able to help me develop within the company.
- There should be a salary increase of at least £100 per month.
- In my future position I must be able to spend at least 50% of my time on executive activities.

Step 4 Judging attainability
Only now will you be able to judge whether the plan is attainable or not. It is not useful to judge the attainability sooner. Only after steps 1 to 3 will you have a clear view of the target, and only then can you judge whether it is attainable or not.

■ **Example of the four-step method:**
- I want to lose 40 pounds because at the moment I am 40 pounds over the weight appropriate to my height, and my doctor tells me I run a health risk. I notice that I run out of breath quickly. My uncle Joe was also far too heavy, and he died young. I am deeply ashamed of my belly when walking on the beach and even when I just stand under the shower (= being specific: note that the personal motivation is very clear too).
- I want to have reached my target before summer (because I want to be trim when I go to the beach); therefore, if I start in January, I will have to lose 8 pounds per month (=subdividing).
- I will do it by jogging an hour each day and by following the so-called 'bread diet' (= subdividing).
- I will weigh myself each week and will check each month whether I have lost a minimum of 8 pounds (= making measurable).
- I will keep it up because I will jog together with a good friend. My condition will also improve through jogging, and that will motivate me to keep it up. Also, an hour a day is not much. The fun part of a bread diet is that some days you can eat a lot, so that the days on which you eat only bread become more bearable. The goal is also very important to me, because being overweight entails a health risk and I am ashamed of my weight. In brief, there is a real chance it will succeed (= judging attainability; here again, the 'personal motivation' is extremely important.

The trick in formulating study targets therefore, is first to determine your weak points or points for improvement and then, based on this step method, to set up a course on improving these points.

Note: With this study target your own motivation is essential. You yourself have to want to lose weight and be convinced that you want to. If Sandy says she is going to lose weight because her husband wants her to, it will fail. And even if Sandy succeeds, she will have done it for the wrong reason: attaining the target will have done her no good because she has no personal investment in the target.

 You can enter the study targets you have formulated as action points in the PDP Action Points section and logbook of the PDP Toolbox. By regularly reflecting on your study targets, you will start to work more effectively and efficiently. Chapter 2.2 tells you how to reflect on your study targets.

6.2 Points of action and logbook

This section represents an extension of Section 6.1 and may be refererred to when you do various assignments.

Sometimes a study target is quickly identified: a hothead can on occasion think that he 'wants to become more patient'. A study target like this can be made more specific and measurable by using the four-step method (see Section 6.1), but as long as you do not describe your behaviour specifically it remains a vague target. How often are you still impatient? How often are you truly patient? What are your specific experiences?

The 'logbook self-evaluation' is a simple tool for this. During a specified period (e.g. two weeks) you will write down all the experiences relating to those study targets. You will thus record exactly what went well and what did not. According to Quinn (2003, p. 152) a logbook like this is an aid to one's self-development. After all, writing forces you to record your experiences in precise terms and this alone will force you to reflect carefully on it.

The following represents an imaginary example of a logbook: it is William Wormwood's logbook. He has set up study targets before starting a student project and he will now keep a logbook for a week. In the same way you can record your progress in relation to your study targets. Do this after consulting your teacher or tutor. The logbook will cover a longer period and will contain more examples.

On the basis of this chart William Wormwood needs to make a report evaluating his progress: will he be satisfied or not on the basis of this report, and why?

 You can enter the action points and behavioural goals you have formulated in the PDP Action Points section and logbook of the PDP Toolbox and also record your progress.

Description of behaviour targets	Date	Description	Evaluation
Punctuality: check deadlines, prepare in advance	February 4	15 minutes late for the project team meeting	The team was upset and that upset me too.
	February 6	Finished my assignments for the team correctly and on time!	The tutor complimented me and I was quite satisfied as well.
	February 7	Forgot meeting with the tutor. Result: badly prepared.	Waste of time: the conversation was about nothing! Stupid!
	February 7	For the first time in my life finished all my homework for microeconomics.	I understood the lecture much better than usual.
Patience	February 5	Got awfully upset because Charles did not understand me.	Futile quarrel: about nothing. Not good for the final result either.
	February 6	Gave a good account of my assignments, without getting angry.	A good businesslike discussion: input was praised during evaluation.
	February 6	Lost my temper because the meeting lasted too long.	Stupid: I should have stayed calm. Now the atmosphere is ruined.
	February 7	Did assignment 4b together with Peter. We disagreed, but came up with a good compromise.	Very satisfied: the compromise was better than my own solution and I did not get angry.

6.3   Giving feedback

Giving feedback is dealt with in Assignments 4.1 to 4.7; that is, in nearly all assignments in Chapter 4.

Here we give ten rules of thumb for giving feedback.

1 Say what you have actually observed, without judgment or interpretation, as an 'I-message'.
'You talk so uninterestingly' sounds like an attack – the other person will go into defensive mode or will not take the feedback seriously. Even worse is: 'You were not interested at all when you told me that', or 'you could not be bothered to get me interested in it, so I fell asleep'. The following is better: 'When you told me that story I had problems staying interested. I lost the drift mainly because I did not get enough specific examples'. In this way you are not passing judgment or interpreting, but merely giving your personal observations. It sounds far less 'attacking'. Also, remember not to speak on behalf of others. 'We all think that...' is more attacking than 'I think that...'

2   Give your feedback as specifically as possible: focus your feedback on behaviour or results, not on the person or his character. Limit yourself to what the others can digest and do not generalise.

'You are always so dominant!' sounds like a personal attack. It is better to say 'I thought you monopolised the discussion'. A comment of this type is an 'I-message' (see above) and you also describe specific behaviour. The latter is especially important: If someone is told he is domineering he will not know what he should change; If someone is told that he 'talks too much' he will know. You specify your feedback by zooming in on someone else's behaviour ('talking too much') or performance. Specific feedback is productive feedback – feedback that is useful to the other person.

3   Stick to the here and now (do not talk about things past).

Do not discuss things from the past: do not offer criticism such as 'Two years ago you didn't do enough either'. Your memories of the events are surely different from those of your fellow student, and neither of you can recall exactly what happened then. Result: useless bickering about something that is not even relevant anymore.

4   Choose the right moment ('timing') and do not make a fool of the other person.

Sticking to the 'here and now' means you are giving your feedback in a timely fashion. Do not be in a hurry either: sometimes it is better to wait awhile. You could choose to have a one-to-one talk, so that the other person does not lose face in front of the whole group. Sometimes you should wait until someone has cooled off. Sometimes you also should wait for your own anger to subside.

5   Give positive feedback too.

Feedback is more than just criticism! Positive, appreciative remarks are excellent feedback. Sometimes it is a good idea to combine criticism with positive feedback: first indicate what you appreciate and then state your criticism. This softens the criticism. For example: 'I found the first part of your presentation very clear. You also injected a lot of enthusiasm into it, but in the second part I lost the thread and your enthusiasm was considerably less as well'. Finally, remember that positive feedback must also be specific (see rule of thumb 2). 'I think you are very constructive' is not specific enough. It is better to say: 'I think you motivate all of us by coming up with so many ideas and because you are always cheerful'. Then the receiver of feedback will know what you mean by 'constructive'.

6   Do not overload the receiver – limit yourself to the most important things.

It is unwise to state ten points of criticism giving five examples per point: your fellow student will not get the information he needs. He may also close up because he is swamped by criticism. Limit yourself to the most important things. Be brief and concise.

7 Indicate the effect the other person has on you (do not give advice on what he should have done).
Example: 'Just now, you did not react to my comments on your work, instead you were sharing a joke with Jack. I got irritated and angry because I felt ignored and I thought you were laughing at my comments'. Now the other person knows exactly what the effect of his behaviour was. He knows you are angry and why. Compare this to incorrect feedback: 'You'd better not sit there laughing like that because you come across as very arrogant!' The other person knows that you are angry, but without understanding why. He does not understand your feedback. And what can he do with feedback he does not understand?

8 Only state your opinion after explaining what the effect on you was.
For rule of thumb 1 we have already indicated that you must be careful with assessments, and in rule of thumb 7 we advised you to mention the effect in particular. But sometimes it is necessary to pronounce judgment – when, for example, you think that something is really out of order. But do indicate exactly what is wrong. Do not generalise (see rule of thumb 2), specify the effect (see rule of thumb 7) and only then give the assessment as an I-message (see rule of thumb 1). For example: 'You have not done the six points of action you were supposed to and that is why I cannot continue with my points of action. I find that annoying [= specifying the effect]. I don't think you should do this to the group either: you promised something and you should keep your promise'.

9 Criticise in the form of a wish, if necessary.
Rule of thumb 7 states you should be careful with giving advice. Yet it is good to indicate specifically what you would like to see changed. Instead of 'I found the story boring' you could say 'I thought your story was really a bit boring. It would be livelier and clearer if you were to incorporate more specific examples'. With 'lazybones' your fellow student can do nothing, but he can do something with: 'You have not done the six points of action you were supposed to execute and that is why I cannot continue with my points of action. I find that rather annoying [= specifying the effect]. I don't think you can do this to the group either [= assessment]. I would appreciate it if by the next meeting you have completed these six points of action [= wish].

10 Always check whether the other has understood his feedback.
Last but not least, it is highly advisable to check if the other person has understood what you have said. At least ask him what he thinks of your comments, and pursue your questioning if necessary. Try to get the other person to summarise your feedback in his own words. Listen closely to his response. A check like that is necessary as even well-meant feedback may not come across in the way you intended, mainly because criticism frightens some people.

6.4   Receiving feedback

Nearly all assignments in Chapter 4 and Assignments 2.5, 3.3, 3.4, 3.5 and 3.9 deal with receiving feedback. Receiving feedback requires active listening. Section 6.5 contains instructions on active listening.

Here follow six rules of thumb for the proper receiving of feedback.

1   View feedback as a chance to learn and not as an attack.
This is more an attitude than a skill – do not view feedback as a personal attack. Take it seriously and show that – keep looking at the other, react seriously. Summarise the feedback in your own words. Do not let the criticism get you down – everyone can make mistakes; you as well.

2   Do not be defensive.
Do not defend yourself ('Yes, okay, but I didn't have time because...'), do not contradict the other person. Do not 'hit back' by exclaiming 'Yes, but you don't do anything either'. Do not respond in an injured way. Always let the person giving feedback finish.

3   Do not explain without really listening and without responding to the change that is called for.
Do not hit back. React to the feedback by dealing with the content. For example: 'So you think I did not give enough input during the last two meetings and you want me to prepare better and provide more input for the next meeting [= summarising the feedback, dealing with the change that is called for]. You are right – I could have prepared myself better. So okay, I will be better prepared for the next meeting'. If necessary, you can then briefly (note well!) explain how it came about. But always deal with the criticism and the changes called for.

4   Ask for clarification on things you do not understand.
Sometimes feedback is too vague or too general. Ask for an explanation and especially for specific examples. Do that with positive feedback as well – it would be a pity if compliments did not come across properly. Listen attentively, summarise the feedback in your own words and in the event of uncertainty ask for specific examples. Make sure the feedback is as specific as possible. Ask for examples and clarification, otherwise the feedback will be worthless.

5   Deal seriously with the part of the criticism you agree with.
Point 3 mentions dealing seriously with the part of the criticism you agree with. You might say: 'You are right; I could have done more preparation. So okay, the next meeting I will be better prepared... ' If you receive three points of criticism of which you think one is correct, do not forget to deal with that point. You may protest against the two invalid (to your mind) points of criticism, as long as you indicate that you do something about what you see as a valid point of criticism.

6 Thank the person giving feedback for his trouble.
Understand that it is difficult to give good feedback so a word of thanks is only polite. Also, do not forget to accept appreciative feedback with 'thank you'. If you fail to react to a compliment at all (or with awkward remarks such as 'oh yeah, maybe...') you will lessen the chance of people complimenting you again.

6.5   Active listening

Active listening is a skill that is crucial to receiving feedback. All assignments requiring the receiving of feedback (see Section 6.4) require this skill. This skill is also essential to interview success (see Section 6.6).

Active listening may be defined as follows:
The student shows he is capable of gleaning important information from spoken statements. An essential part of this is continued questioning and dealing with responses.

'Active listening' is an important skill: someone who is a bad listener is also bad in receiving feedback. Management, analysing problems, coaching and working with others all require the ability to listen actively. All higher education professions demand such skills and as such it is wise to learn to listen well while you are training for a profession.

Here are eight rules of thumb for active listening:
1 Let the other person finish speaking.
2 Show interest in the other person's input by your attitude and behaviour.
3 Give others room to express an opinion or idea.
4 Keep asking questions about the information given.
5 Ask for clarification, reason or cause if you do not understand the other person properly.
6 Briefly summarise what has been said.
7 Take account of the spirit in which things are said.
8 Regularly check to see if you have properly understood what the other person said.
9 Refer to what has been mentioned by others earlier.

6.6   The interview

To glean information from others you may elect to interview them. Assignments 3.7 and 5.9 deal with conducting interviews. Here are some instructions for conducting a good interview.

The person interviewed
Determine who you are going to interview and why; know exactly what you want more information about. Prepare the questions leading to your goal. Prepare the content: first read all information you can find on the person you want to interview – what profession

does he have and for which company or organisation does he work? If you want to interview a manager, for example, first read a book or an article on management. That information will help improve your list of questions and will allow you to pursue them better during the interview.

Types of questions
As you prepare for the interview, pay attention to the sort of questions you want to put. Questions fall into various categories:

Open questions

Open questions allow the person interviewed freedom in his answers. For example: 'What are the nice parts of your job?' The advantage is that you do not push the person interviewed in a specific direction; this will keep him at ease. The disadvantage is that he can go off at a tangent. Consequently, open questions should be somewhat pointed ('Tell me about yourself' is too open), and may need to lead to further questions (open, but sometimes restricted as well).

Restricted questions

Restricted questions offer the person interviewed a choice from a limited number of alternatives. For example: 'Do you actually like your job or would you prefer to be doing something else?' The pointedness is the main advantage; sometimes you have to force someone to give a clear-cut answer. Another advantage is that people who have problems expressing themselves or who are introverted can do with a nudge. If they are not nudged they may simply not say anything. The disadvantage is that nudging may be construed as too intrusive.

Direct questions

With direct questions you aim straight for your target (the information desired). For example: 'Are you satisfied with the work?' Or, 'Do you find your training links up directly to your profession?' The directness is an advantage; a disadvantage is that direct questions may come across as impertinent.

Indirect questions

With indirect questions you do not go straight for your target because it may be too painful or confrontational. For example: 'What are the nice parts of your job?' Or, if you suspect the person interviewed works far too hard: 'How much spare time do you have each day?' Or if you think someone is fed up with his job but does not dare to say so: 'Can you enumerate the nicest aspects of working with this company? Are there things in your company you are less pleased with? And so on.

Tip: ask open and indirect questions at the beginning of the interview to put the person interviewed at his ease. Later you can ask restricted and direct questions for exact information. Pursue the questions during the interview.

Ways of pursuing questions
After each answer from the person interviewed, ask yourself if you now know enough or not. If not, pursue the question, especially with points that are important to your goal. Pursuing questions is a good way of avoiding ending up with answers that are too vague, and thus not helpful in reaching the goal of the interview.

Pursuing questions

Here are a number of good pursuing techniques:

- *Give summaries or conclusions in your own words, followed by a question.* For example: 'If I understand you correctly, you find your job varied; is that right?' Another example: 'All in all I get the impression you are disappointed in the project; is that correct? Could you explain precisely what you found disappointing?' In this way you will encourage the person interviewed. Your summaries show that you have listened to him attentively and enable you to check if you have understood him correctly. You can politely interrupt someone who is talking too much. Summarise his answer, ask 'is that right?' and when he answers in the affirmative, you can proceed to the next point.
- *Repeat part of the answer (a word, sentence, part of a sentence) in a questioning tone.* By doing so you invite the person interviewed to say more on the subject. This may be useful if the subject was not dealt with comprehensively, or if the person interviewed strayed from the subject.
- *Ask for clarification.* Repeat part of a sentence and ask: 'In what way did you mean that?' You can also introduce a hypothetical situation: 'You said you would never sign an anti-Jewish declaration, but suppose you miss out on a major order in Saudi Arabia because of that?'
- *Ask for specific examples – especially in matters important to you.* Often people's answers are too general. Force them to be specific. After all, only specific information is any good to you. If someone says: 'I have a busy job', you will still not know very much. You will know more if somebody tells you he works 80 hours a week and describes two of his busy workdays. He will only do that if you ask: 'Busy, you say? How many hours per week do you work?' and 'So you work 80 hours a week? That's a lot! Can you describe what your last two workdays were like?'

Processing the interview

It is useful to record the interview with a dictaphone. Write your report immediately after the interview, when you still remember everything clearly. Do not write down all answers verbatim, but summarise them and only write down the most noteworthy quotes. In the report deal with the information that is relevant to you. Indicate which were the most important, instructive and informative answers to your questions.

You will find more information on conducting an interview in Grit (2000), Chapter 7: Conducting an interview, and Hulshof (2001).

6.7   Time management

Why do some people do lots of work and accomplish a lot, whilst others seem to accomplish hardly anything at all for the same amount of work? Are you one of those for whom an hour, a day, a week seems to have flown by? The exam that seemed so distant is the day after tomorrow, and you still have to study a lot for it. The deadline for handing in the report is approaching awfully quickly.

Here are some tips and exercises for time management.

- Begin each day by setting up a schedule for that day. This will take ten minutes at the most and can save you a lot of time. If you buy a large format diary you can write down a detailed list of activities for each day.
- Write down the list of activities with a minus sign (–) in front of each one. When you have completed the activity, turn the minus sign into a plus sign (+). Your list of minus signs will thus change into plus signs during the day. This has a positive effect (literally!). At the end of the day you will see at a glance what you have spent your time on.
- Also write down reminders relating to future events. If you have a meeting about an important report in a fortnight, note the time of the meeting and also put in a reminder that in twelve days' time you must have read the report. Do not just enter the date of a birthday in your diary, write down a reminder to buy a present three days ahead of time. That is, plan the preparation of important events as well. If you do this you will not end up being short of time.

ASAP

- Try to complete new business as soon as possible. Do things ASAP (*as soon as possible*). If you write the minutes of a meeting immediately after it you may need less than an hour. If you wait for a week, it will take you at least twice as long. Putting off activities nearly always costs extra time.
- Plan one or more tasks for each day that you will be able to finish. Then, at the end of the day, you will not have the feeling of not having done anything.
- Preferably do boring but necessary chores first.
- Do difficult things at times when you are feeling fit. This is in the morning for most people. After a meal you are less capable of doing complicated things – your body is busy digesting the food.
- Have only brief contacts with others when you are busy. An awful lot of time is 'chatted away'. That can be a lot of fun, but it may heighten your stress level when you are busy. If someone asks you for help, do not immediately say yes. Think whether you have time for it or not.
- Be reliable in keeping appointments. Only make promises that you can fulfil. Otherwise you will be wasting your own and other people's time.
- Make a habit of being on time for appointments and try to get others to do the same. If four people have to wait a quarter of an hour for someone else, an hour will have been wasted.
- Try to do things properly the first time and try to make as few mistakes as possible. Preventing one mistake could cost you a few minutes. Making up for a mistake may cost you half a day. Of course, you must not be excessively afraid of making mistakes otherwise you will not accomplish anything.
- Try to pre-empt problems. Solving a problem takes time too.
- Do not make things more attractive than necessary. Students often spend a lot of effort on the cover of a report or project while the teacher would be satisfied with a simple cover fastened with staples. By the way, this is often flight behaviour: it is easier to make a good cover than a report with good contents.

- Choose the meetings you plan to attend. You do not have to be everywhere. Not all meetings and not even all parties are worthwhile.
- Only read paper work that is interesting. A lot of paper may reach your desk. Much of it is uninteresting and can go straight into the wastepaper bin. Do it right away. If you do not throw them away, you will pick up the same papers time and again and only be moving them from one pile to the next.
- Keep a clean work surface. When you ask some people for a specific document they know exactly where to find it – somewhere in a three-foot high pile. Being unable to find things costs a lot of time. Store important documents in folders with a clear title and dividers. The time invested in cleaning things up is quickly made up.
- Using e-mail may save you a lot of time: after all, the other person is always available. However unnecessary use may cost a lot of time. Everybody sends each other copies of everything that is sent. When using e-mail, set rules on what can be sent and what absolutely not. Managers' mailboxes may overflow because every employee sends them a copy of everything just to show how hard he is working.
- A mobile phone is very handy – you can always be reached. But do you want to be? Phoning takes time and being phoned can be very disturbing when you are doing something important. Give your mobile phone number only to people that may phone you any time. There will probably not be too many, and you can always switch off a mobile phone!
- Take time to relax regularly. Do not skip breaks, even when busy. Work on keeping fit.
- Be positive when approaching others. It is hard to accomplish anything with your fellow students or colleagues in an atmosphere of grumbling. When a colleague has tackled a problem in the wrong way, a remark such as: 'You made the mistake and it's up to you to correct it' will certainly upset him and make him refuse to help you. If you ask him 'to have another look at the chosen solution' you will be showing your respect and this will make him more motivated. Bear in mind that most people take unkindly to criticism. Also see Section 6.3 on giving feedback.

6.8   The letter of application

At the end of your studies you will apply for a job, usually by writing a letter of application. Each letter of application must be accompanied by a curriculum vitae often abbreviated to CV: a description of your working life. The assignments you have done in this book are a source of information for your CV. Include only the positive points.
In this section we will give a number of tips you can use in writing your letter of application. These tips are not exhaustive – there are thick tomes wholly devoted to job applications. Use the Internet and a search engine with suitable key words to get further information and tips on applying for a job.

These tips are also worth bearing in mind when you apply for an internship.

- The aim of a letter of application is to sell yourself and be invited for a job interview.
- Firstly, do some research on the company you want to work for.
  - Use annual reports, the library and the Internet for this.
  - If possible, pay a visit to a branch of the company to sample the atmosphere.
  - Contact people you know who work for this company.
- A popular layout for a letter of application consists of:
  - *Introduction*. In this part you should state the reason for your letter, the situation you are applying for and why you are applying.
  - *Core*. In this part you discuss the job qualifications stated in the vacancy advertisement and your qualities.
  - *Conclusion*. In this part you are trying to set up a meeting/ interview.
- Try to find out who the letter should be addressed to. Try phoning the company (reception) to obtain the name plus initials (and title) of the relevant person in Human Resources. When writing the letter, put yourself in the place of the reader. Try to imagine yourself in his situation.
- Make your letter sufficiently original. The Human Resources department receives a lot of letters. Your letter must stand out in a positive sense. So do not simply copy a letter from a study book. This would be fatal. Rephrase an opening sentence such as: 'Regarding your vacancy offer...' and by all means avoid a concluding sentence such as 'Awaiting your response, I remain'. Do not overdo it with your originality, however: the letter should be appropriate to the type of company. If the letter could just as easily come from another student its tone and contents are probably too impersonal and need adjusting.
- Make it clear in your letter why you are applying to that company specifically. Try to demonstrate your interest by listing activities you have undertaken in the past. If you could send your letter to another company without changing anything, the letter is too general.
- In an open application state which position you would like to have in the company. Why are you interested, and what kind of a job would you like?
- Your letter should preferably not be longer than one page, and certainly no more than two pages!
- Do not include information in the letter that also can be found in your CV.
- Be succint and avoid grandiose claims.
- Your letter and CV must give an indication of what kind of person you are. Do not be too modest: it is better to be a touch arrogant. Try to exude confidence and avoid phrases such as 'I hope...' and 'perhaps...'.
- Have your letter checked by someone else, preferably an experienced teacher.

6.9   Your curriculum vitae

A curriculum vitae (CV) is a document accompanying a letter of application. It is a systematic compilation of your personal data. Refer to your personality and competency profiles to write it. You could structure your CV as follows:

Personal data
- First name
- Surname
- Address
- Post code and town/city
- Telephone numbers
- E-mail address
- Nationality
- Gender
- Date of birth
- Marital status (married, unmarried)
- Driver's licence
- You could include a scanned photograph.
- ...

Education and courses
- Duration
- Education
- Name(s) of the school/institution
- Place
- Result

Work experience such as work, part-time jobs and internships
- Name and location of the organisation
- Your position
- Duration
- Other information

Other information
- Relevant strong points from your personality profile
- Special competencies
- Languages
- Relevant computer skills
- Special projects (at school, work)
- Relevant hobbies, such as chairmanships, member of school paper editorial team, referee

References
Name, position, company and phone numbers of people from your school or previous jobs who know you well and are willing to provide positive information about you. First ask them for permission, because they may be called.

6.10   The job interview

Once you have managed to be invited for a job interview, you have to think of the following things:

- Prepare yourself for the job interview. Make it clear you have previously made inquiries about the company. Use the same sources for this as enumerated in Section 6.8.
- Make notes in advance.
    - What do you want to know about the company?
    - What do you want to say about yourself?
    - What are you good at?
    - What are you interested in? Try to demonstrate your interest.
    - What position would you like to have?
    - What relevant skills and competencies do you have?
    - Explain the procedure if your application is for an internship. You will find it in the internship manual. Read this manual in advance carefully so that you will be able to answer all questions. Take the manual along for the interview.
    - Try to prepare yourself for questions that may be put to you:
        - Why do you want to work for, or have an internship with this company?
        - Why are you in particular a suitable candidate?
        - Are you a good team worker?
    - You may be asked to prove the answers you have given, for example: 'What shows us you are independent?' et cetera.
- No-one will mind you showing up for a job interview neatly dressed but they may mind if you are not.
- Take pen and paper so that you can make notes of what is said during the interview.
- Make sure to bring your CV and letter of application along with you.
- On entering, shake hands firmly and clearly introduce yourself to all people present. Make sure your hands are not moist.
- Look at all the people present during your introduction and the conversation. Be aware of your posture as well.
- Put notes you have made in advance on the table.
- After concluding the interview, ask for a tour of the company.
- Try to set up another meeting.

6.11   Networking

Increasingly, job openings are not being filled in the traditional way. Instead of a company posting an opening that you could apply for, openings are being filled by means of personal networks. It is therefore important for you to invest personally in business relations. Keep in touch with the company of your internship or the company you visited during an excursion. Attend congresses and lectures. Once people know you, they will be willing to do things for you. And perhaps they will think of you first when an opening comes up.

Literature

Belbin, R.M. (1999). *Managementteams. Over succes- en faalfactoren voor teams*. Schoonhoven: Academic Service.

Belbin, R.M. (1999). *Teamrollen op het werk*. Schoonhoven: Academic Service.

Boekaerst M, et al (1998). *Leren en instructie*. Assen: Van Gorcum.

Bonnstetter, B.J., Suiter, J.I. & Widrick, R.J. (1993). *The universal language disc*. Target Training International.

Braas, C., et al (2001). *Taaltopics Vergaderen*. Groningen: Wolters-Noordhoff.

Cameron, S. (2007). *Vaardigheden voor studie en loopbaan*. Amsterdam: Pearson Education Benelux.

Covey, Stephen R. (2002). *De zeven eigenschappen van effectief leiderschap*. Amsterdam: Amstel Uitgevers.

Covey, Sean (2005). *Zeven eigenschappen die jou succesvol maken!* Amsterdam: Amstel Uitgevers.

Covey, Sean (2006). Zeven eigenschappen die jou succesvol maken! Werkboek. Amsterdam: Amstel Uitgevers.

Gramsbergen-Hoogland, Y., et al (1999). *Persoonlijke kwaliteit*. Groningen: Wolters-Noordhoff.

Grit, R. (2003). *Project management*. Groningen: Wolters-Noordhoff.

Grit, R. (2002). *Informatiemanagement*. Groningen: Wolters-Noordhoff.

Grit, R., Guit, R., Sijde, N. van der (2006). *Sociaal competent*. Groningen: Wolters-Noordhoff.

Grit, R., Gerritsma, M. (2007). *Competent adviseren*. Groningen: Wolters-Noordhoff.

Grit, R., Geus, J.W. de (2006). *Management en logistiek*. Groningen: Wolters-Noordhoff.

Hulshof, M. (2001). *Leren interviewen*. Groningen: Wolters-Noordhoff.

Kalkman, H., et al (2003). *MDI-profielen Handboek*. Amsterdam: MDI-instituut.

Koeleman, H. (2003). *Interne communicatie als managementinstrument*. Alphen aan den Rijn/Diegem: Kluwer.

Kolb, D. (1998). *Leren en instructie*. Assen: Van Gorcum.

Ofman, D. (2000). *De kernkwaliteiten van het enneagram*. Schiedam: Scriptum.

Ofman, D. (2002). *Bezieling en kwaliteit in organisaties*. Schiedam: Kosmos.

Oomkes, F.R. (1989). *Communicatieleer*. Amsterdam/Meppel: Boom.

Oomkes, F.R. (1998). *Training als beroep* (CD-Rom). Amsterdam/Meppel: Boom.

Quinn, R.E. (2003). *Handboek Managementvaardigheden*. Den Haag: Academic Service.

Reijnders, E. (1997). *Interne communicatie: aanpak en achtergronden*. Assen: Van Gorcum.

Ruymbeke, B.P.E.M. van, et al (1987). *Omgangskunde in theorie en praktijk*. Rijswijk: Nijgh en Van Ditmar.

Websites

www.competentiemanagement.noordhoff.nl
www.sociaalcompetent.noordhoff.nl
www.poptoolbox.nl
www.roelgrit.nl
www.roelgrit.noordhoff.nl/
www.noordhoff.nl
www.123test.nl
www.carrieretijger.nl
www.thesis.nl
www.mijnkernkwaliteiten.nl
competentiemanagement.pagina.nl
www.hbo-raad.nl
www.mdi.nl
solliciteren.pagina.nl

Appendix 1 **Installing and using the PDP Toolbox**

Website www.managingyourcompetencies.nl
This book is supported by a website containing various documents and
the necessary software for the PDP Toolbox (see Section 1.4).

Documents
The website contains the following documents that are useful for a
number of assignments in this book:
· Checklist self-evaluation (Appendix 3)
· Checklist evaluation fellow group members (Appendix 4)
· Group roles (Appendix 5)

The PDP Toolbox
The PDP Toolbox is a database program containing tools for setting up
your personal development plan and for updating your portfolio.

Installation
Prior to use you must install the PDP Toolbox on a storage medium such
as a hard disk. You have to download the program software from the
website. When you start the downloaded program via Windows explorer,
this installation program will ask where you want to install the PDP
Toolbox. You can do this in various places:
· *Hard disk*. Install the program on the hard disk of your PC or
  notebook.
· *Memory stick*. You can put a memory stick in the USB port of a PC.
  The memory stick shows as an extra disk on *This Computer*. You can
  take a memory stick anywhere and connect it to another PC with a
  suitable USB port. Start the program PDP.EXE and continue. However,
  a memory stick is a bit slower than a hard disk.
· *Computer network*. If your school or college permits it, the program can
  be installed once on a full computer network. Using a suitable link,
  you can save your data on a CD or on your own part of the network.

Securing your data
Type in your password in the Personality Profile section of the program.
For security reasons you will have to type in the password twice. If you
do not use a password, anybody with access to your PC can retrieve your
data. If you have entered a password, on starting the Toolbox a window
will appear in which you will have to type your password to gain access
to the program.

Take care not to forget your password otherwise your data will no longer
be accessible!

Data output
Thanks to a menu option in the PDP Toolbox you can simply copy your
data onto a disk and give that to your teacher. He then has access to your
data via his Toolbox.

Back-up
Make sure to make a back-up of the data in your PDP Toolbox – it can be found in the Popdata folder. This is important in the event of a hard disk crash or diskette malfunction: you will have lost all your precious data. The pop archive folder contains the documents you have copied using the saving function of the PDP Toolbox.

Assignments 1.1, 1.2, 1.3 and 1.4 contain an introduction to the operation of the PDP Toolbox.

The PDP Toolbox has an extended help function, which you can access via the F1 key. You will also find help buttons in the windows of the program. At the time of installation of the program, a manual is also installed. You will find this as a separate file on the website.

Appendix 2 **Learning styles test**

This test forms part of Assignment 2.10, Personal learning styles test. It is derived from Kolb (1998).

This test deals with learning in the broadest sense of the word. It consists of nine rows of four statements. You fill in the numbers 1, 2, 3 and 4 across each row. Each number only occurs once in each row. There are no right or wrong answers.

Complete the test according to the following instructions:
· Read the statements in each horizontal row.
· Assign an order of merit to each statement, using the numbers 1 to 4:
    1 the statement least appropriate to your way of learning
    2 the statement that is a poor match with your way of learning
    3 the statement that almost matches your way of learning
    4 the statement that is most appropriate to your way of learning
· Fill in the numbers according to the instructions under the chart.
· Enter the numbers in the graph.
· Connect the points with straight lines.
· The quadrant with the largest surface is your dominant style of learning.

a ☐ You are selective about the information you take in.	☐ You explore the situation first.	☐ You get involved when a problem occurs.	☐ Practical exercise is important to you.
b ☐ You are open to new things.	☐ Relevance is your starting-point.	☐ You analyse the situation.	☐ You react neutrally and do not take a position.
c ☐ You pay attention to what you yourself and others feel.	☐ You look at the situation and note what you see.	☐ You reflect a lot.	☐ You want to take action; action means progress.
d ☐ You accept things the way they are.	☐ You like to take risks.	☐ You take a position and judge accordingly.	☐ You consciously try to deal with the situation.
e ☐ You like to work intuitively.	☐ You are mainly production-orientated.	☐ You like to think logically.	☐ You are always asking questions.
f ☐ You think abstraction and conceptualisation are important.	☐ You view yourself as mainly reflective.	☐ You believe that things cannot be concrete enough.	☐ You take an active stance.
g ☐ You are focused mainly on what happens today.	☐ You regularly reflect on events.	☐ You are mainly future-orientated.	☐ You deal with problems pragmatically.
h ☐ Gaining experience is important to you.	☐ You observe the situation and gather data.	☐ You form a cohesive conceptual framework.	☐ You try solutions and experiment.
i ☐ You experience events intensely.	☐ You prefer to be reserved.	☐ You deal rationally with situations and problems.	☐ You feel responsible for what happens.
Column total ☐ b+c+d+e+g+h	☐ a+c+f+g+h+i	☐ b+c+d+e+h+i	☐ a+c+f+g+h+i
Concrete experience	Reflective observation	Abstract thinking	Active experimentation

Concrete experience

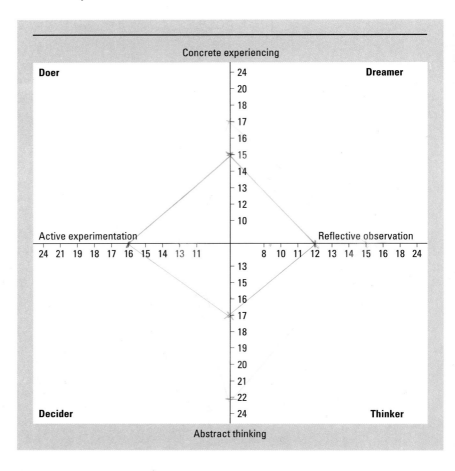

Appendix 3 **Checklist: Self-evaluation**

Just as Appendix 5, this appendix forms part of Assignment 4.1. Circle your score for each statement (1 = lowest score, 4 = highest score). Give yourself a total score (on a scale from 1 to 10).

Your name:

Year: **Group:**

Statement	Disagree		Agree	
1 I prepare well for the meeting by completing all assignments.	1	2	3	4
2 I often voice my opinions.	1	2	3	4
3 I know how to explain my opinions to others.	1	2	3	4
4 I listen attentively to the opinions of others.	1	2	3	4
5 I do not force my opinions on others; I look for a compromise.	1	2	3	4
6 I like to take the initiative (doing the final steps, etc).	1	2	3	4
7 I propose a lot of good ideas.	1	2	3	4
8 I am enthusiastic.	1	2	3	4
9 I contribute positively to the general atmosphere (jokes, compliments, etc).	1	2	3	4
10 I am not afraid of criticising someone (with respect to content or procedure).	1	2	3	4
11 I admit my mistakes.	1	2	3	4
12 I keep my appointments punctually.	1	2	3	4
13 I am flexible.	1	2	3	4

My total score (1 minimum, 10 maximum)

Appendix 4 **Checklist: Evaluation of fellow group members**

Just like Appendix 5, this appendix forms part of Assignment 4.1. For each statement circle the score you give to each of your fellow group members (1 = lowest score, 4 = highest score). Give each member a total score (on a scale from 1 to 10).

Name group member				
Year:		**Group:**		
Statement	**Disagree**		**Agree**	
1 He/she prepares well for the meeting by completing all assignments.	1	2	3	4
2 He/she often voices his/her opinion.	1	2	3	4
3 He/she knows how to explain his/her opinion to others.	1	2	3	4
4 He/she listens attentively to the points of view of others.	1	2	3	4
5 He/she does not force his/her opinion on others; he/she looks for a compromise.	1	2	3	4
6 He/she likes to take the initiative (doing the final steps, etc.).	1	2	3	4
7 He/she introduces many good ideas.	1	2	3	4
8 He/she is enthusiastic.	1	2	3	4
9 He/she contributes positively to the general atmosphere (jokes, compliments, etc).	1	2	3	4
10 He/she is not afraid of criticising someone (with respect to content or procedure).	1	2	3	4
11 He/she admits his/her mistakes.	1	2	3	4
12 He/she keeps appointments punctually.	1	2	3	4
13 He/she is flexible.	1	2	3	4

Total score group member (1 minimum, 10 maximum).

Appendix 5 **Group roles**

This appendix (inspired by Van Ruymbeke, 1987) forms part of Assignment 4.5.

Group roles for group member / Group roles	Name group member	Name	Group member 1	Group member 2	Group member 3	Group member 4	Group member 5	Group member 6	Group member 7	Group member 8	Group member 9	Group member 10
A												
Originator of ideas												
Analytic												
Leader												
Planner												
Summariser												
Decider												
Coordinator												
Action-instigator												
B												
Pace-setter												
Motivator												
Comedian												
Good listener												
Atmosphere setter												
Helper												
Conflict mediator												
Faithful follower												
Theorist												
Practical person												
Specialist												
C												
Domineering person												
Problem-maker												
Searching for recognition												
Deviator (wayward ideas)												
Creative person												
Blocker (obstructs decision-making)												
Quarrel-picker												
Controller (stickler for details)												

Appendix 6 **Styles of communication**

With permission, this test is taken from Oomkes (1998) and forms part of Assignment 4.5.

You will be given statements in pairs. Each time, circle the statement that is most characteristic for you. These statements are not opposites. Choose quickly and spontaneously. There are no right or wrong answers. Determine your score at the end.

Statements

[1] I like action *or*
[2] I tackle problems systematically.

[3] I believe teams accomplish more than individuals *or*
[4] I am very keen on innovation.

[5] The future interests me more than the past *or*
[6] I like working with people.

[7] I like to prepare for meetings meticulously *or*
[8] I take appointments very seriously.

[9] I dislike lazing about and wasting time *or*
[10] New ideas must be tested before they are implemented.

[11] I find working with people stimulating *or*
[12] I am always looking for new possibilities.

[13] I want to determine my own goals *or*
[14] When I start something I finish it.

[15] I try to understand the feelings of others *or*
[16] I challenge people around me to perform well.

[17] I think my achievements attract positive feedback *or*
[18] I find a gradual approach works well.

[19] I am good at making contacts *or*
[20] I like solving problems creatively.

[21] I am always drawing conclusions and can foresee future developments
     or
[22] I am sensitive to other people's needs.

[23] Planning is the key to success *or*
[24] I get impatient with extended deliberation.

[25] I become very calm under pressure *or*
[26] I value experience a lot.

[27] I listen to people *or*
[28] People say I am a quick thinker.

[29] Cooperation is a key word for me *or*
[30] I use logical methods to test alternative solutions.

[31] I like tackling different projects at the same time *or*
[32] I am always wondering about things.

[33] I learn by doing *or*
[34] I believe my reason overrules my feelings.

[35] I can predict how others will react in specific situations *or*
[36] I do not like details and prefer to concentrate on the grand design.

[37] Action should always be preceded by analysis *or*
[38] I can sense the atmosphere in a group.

[39] I tend to start things and leave them unfinished *or*
[40] I see myself as a quick decision-maker.

[41] I am always looking for challenging tasks *or*
[42] I trust in observation and in carefully collected data.

[43] I express my feelings well *or*
[44] I like to set up new projects.

[45] I like reading *or*
[46] I see myself as a counsellor.

[47] I prefer doing one thing at a time *or*
[48] I like accomplishing something.

[49] I am fascinated to learn about other people *or*
[50] I like change.

[51] Facts speak for themselves *or*
[52] I use my imagination as much as possible.

[53] I become irascible during long and slowly performed assignments *or*
[54] I am always thinking; my mind never stops working.

[55] Important decisions should be taken with the utmost care *or*
[56] I am convinced people need each other to accomplish something.

[57] I usually make decisions without too much worrying *or*
[58] Feelings always cause problems.

[59] I like it when other people like me *or*
[60] I can solve problems quickly and without mistakes.

[61] I try my new ideas out on others *or*
[62] I believe in a scientific approach.

[63] I like accomplishing things *or*
[64] Good relationships are essential.

[65] I am impulsive *or*
[66] I accept that each person is different.

[67] Communicating with others is a goal in itself *or*
[68] I like intellectual stimulus.

[69] I like to organise *or*
[70] I go from one job to another.

[71] Talking to and working with people is a creative occupation *or*
[72] Self-realisation is a key word for me.

[73] I love playing with ideas *or*
[74] I do not like wasting my time.

[75] I love to do things I am good at *or*
[76] I learn by dealing with other people.

[77] I find abstract ideas interesting *or*
[78] I have an eye for detail.

[79] I like people who can express what they want briefly and concisely *or*
[80] I trust myself.

Determine your score

Determine your score by circling each chosen statement on the following score list. Next, determine the *numbers of circled statements* per style. The maximum possible score is 20 and the collective total for the four styles must be 40.

Score list

Style Action   1-8-9-13-17-24-26-31-33-40-41-48-50-53-57-63-65-70-74-79

Style Tactical 2-7-10-14-18-23-25-30-34-37-42-47-51-55-58-62-66-69-75-78

Style People   3-6-11-15-19-22-27-29-35-38-43-46-49-56-59-64-67-71-76-80

Style Ideas   4-5-12-16-20-21-28-32-36-39-44-45-52-54-60-61-68-72-73-77

The following outline indicates in which phase of your education an assignment is best completed. This is merely a suggestion: consult your teacher to see whether he/she agrees with the sequence. The overview assumes a four-year course. Some assignments can be done more than once. The final column of the chart gives an indication of the time needed for each assignment.

Assign-ment	Title	When?	Sort?	Time
1.1	Introducing the PDP Toolbox	Start of studies	Individually	2 hours
1.2	Description of competencies	Start of studies/more often	Individually	2 hours
1.3	Which competencies will you need to have mastered in the near future?	Start of studies/more often	Individually	1.2 hours
1.4	Recording your study timetabling and assessments	Continually	Individually	1 hour per month
1.5	Gathering documents and evidence	Continually	Individually	
2.1	Steps in self-reflection	Start of studies	Individually	2 hours
2.2	Three phases of your life	Start of studies	Individually	1 hour
2.3	Who do I like, who do I dislike?	Start of studies	Individually	30 minutes
2.4	My big role model	Start of studies/more often	Individually	30 minutes
2.5	Questions to put to friends and acquaintances	Start of studies	Individually	3 hours
2.6	Core qualities	Start of studies/more often	Individually	1 hour
2.7	Enneagram	Start of studies/more often	Individually	1 hour
2.8	Personal values and motives	Start of studies/more often	Individually	2 hours
2.9	Where does my motivation come from?	Start of studies/more often	Individually	1 hour
2.10	Personal learning styles test	Start of studies	Individually	
2.11	Exercises in the applicational learning style	Start of studies	Individually	2 hours
2.12	Exercises in the experiential learning style	Start of studies/more often	Individually/group	2 hours
2.13	Updating your personality profile	Continually	Individually	30 minutes
2.14	Updating your PDP action points and logbook	Continually	Individually	1 hour
3.1	Zero measurement	Start of studies	Individually	2 hours
3.2	Self-reflection half way through the first year of studies	Start of studies	Individually	3 hours
3.3	Introvert or extrovert, thinking or feeling?	From the second year onwards	Individually	1 hour
3.4	Which colour are you?	From the second year onwards	Individually	30 minutes
3.5	Comparing your response behaviour with your basic behaviour	From the first year onwards	Individually	1 hour
3.6	How proactive am I really?	Start of studies/more often	Individually	1-2 hours
3.7	Keeping a logbook on being proactive	Start of studies/more often	Individually	1 hour
3.8	Take the initiative: develop your competencies!	Start of studies/more often	Individually	2 hours
3.9	Formulating a personal mission	Start of studies/more often	Individually	1 hour
3.10	The group's mission and vision: comparing missions	Start of studies/more often	Group	1 hour
3.11	Formulating your targets	Start of studies/more often	Individually	1 hour
3.12	Group targets	Start of studies/more often	Group	1 hour
3.13	Where does my time go?	First or second year	Individually	2 hours
3.14	What type am I?	First and second year	Individually	1 hour
3.15	Establishing priorities	Continually	Individually	1 hour

Assign-ment	Title	When?	Sort?	Time
3.16	Planning your week	Continually	Individually	15 minutes per week
3.17	Implementing the PDCA cycle	Continually	Individually	2 hours
3.18	Learning from your mistakes using the PDCA cycle	Continually	Individually	1-2 hours
3.19	Interviewing an intern	Second or third year	In pairs	3 hours
3.20	Preparation for your internship	Second or third year	In pairs	3 hours
3.21	Self-evaluation after a work-related learning experience	Second or third year	Individually	2 hours
3.22	My motivation	first, second, third (more often)	Individually	1 hour
3.23	Testing your core qualities	Continually	Individually	30 minutes
3.24	Testing your Dublin descriptors	Continually	Individually	1 hour
3.25	Setting up the personality profile	Continually	Individually	1 hour
3.26	Setting up the professional competency profile	Continually	Individually	3 hours
3.27	Updating your personality profile	Continually	Individually	1 hour
3.28	Updating your competencies	Continually	Individually	1 hour
4.1	Evaluating a group	First year (2-3 times)	Group	2 hours
4.2	Evaluating a group of advanced students	From the second year onwards (2-3 times)	Group	2 hours
4.3	Formulating competencies and assessing the group	midway into the first year (2-3×)	Group	2 hours
4.4	Doing the Belbin test	From the second year onwards	Group	1 hour
4.5	Which group role?	From the second year onwards	Group	1 hour
4.6	Which style of communication?	From the second year onwards	Group	2 hours
4.7	Which behaviour?	From the second year onwards	Group	2 hours
4.8	Which team roles?	From the second year onwards	Group	2 hours
4.9	Updating your PDP	From the second year onwards	Group	1 hour
5.1	Employment image	From the second year onwards	Individually	1 hour
5.2	Required competencies	From the second year onwards	Individually	2 hours
5.3	Competencies still to be attained	From the second year onwards	Individually	1 hour
5.4	Jobs on offer research	Third year	Group	3 hours
5.5	The labour market	Third year	Group	2 hours
5.6	Companies in your professional field	Third year	Group	2 hours
5.7	Preparing to go on an excursion	From the second year onwards	Group	3 hours
5.8	The excursion	From the second year onwards	Group	8 hours
5.9	Evaluating the excursion	From the second year onwards	Group	2 hours
5.10	Conducting an interview with a professional	From the second year onwards	Pairs	3 hours
5.11	Presenting the interview	From the second year onwards	Pairs	30 minutes
5.12	Investigating work locations	From the third year onwards	Group	2 hours
5.13	Investigating organisational characteristics	From the third year onwards	Group	2 hours
5.14	Investigating job characteristics	Final year	Group	1 hour
5.15	Minimal job requirements	Final year	Individually	1 hour
5.16	Your dream job	Final year	Individually	1 hour
5.17	Step-by-step plan for getting your dream job	Final year	Individually	30 minutes
5.18	Applying for a job	Final year	Individually	4 hours

Index

About the authors

According to the Belbin test in Section 4.3, a good team consists of members who each play a different Belbin role. That Belbin may be right is apparent from the striking composition of the team of authors that was in a creative but responsible way involved in writing this book. The three authors of this book *Managing your Competencies* (which achieved bestseller status in no time at all) also wrote the book *Sociaal competent*, also published by Noordhoff Uitgevers. Here follows a brief description of the authors.

Drs. Roel Grit (1954) – graduated from Groningen in physical chemistry, is an author for Noordhoff Uitgevers and has written *Project management* and *Informatiemanagement*. Together with other authors he wrote the books *Management en Logistiek* en *Competent adviseren*. For the non-specialist market he wrote *Ontdek de muziek!* published by Unieboek. He teaches project management and information management at various economic and technical institutes. He is closely involved in new developments in the field of teaching. As co-owner of the software company Info/Q automatisation in Emmen, he developed the PDP Toolbox accompanying this book.
Belbin roles: Implementer 53%, Shaper 19% and Completer 17%.

Roelie Guit (1960) – graduated as a drama teacher and worked as a director and actress in the theatre world for a number of years. After coaching students for a long time she is now project leader at the staff agency for educational affairs at the Hanzehogeschool in Groningen. In that function she specializes in the further development of competency-directed teaching.
Belbin roles: Shaper 53%, Team worker 22% and Plant 15%.

Dr. Nico van der Sijde (1959) studied philosophy and literary science in Groningen. His doctoral thesis dealt with the linguistic philosophy of J. Derrida. He has published works on various linguistic philosophical subjects, and has taught at the faculty of arts at Groningen University for some years. He has been teaching communication and general professional skills at the Hogeschool Drenthe since 1997. He also co-ordinated general skills, works as a core teacher in communication & soft skills and was also 'reflection advisor' for Leerbedrijven and SIFE. Since september 2007, he is Advisor at the Hanzehogeschool Groningen.
Belbin roles: Plant 53%, Shaper 22% and Warner 18%.